Better Homes and Gardens®

Container Plants

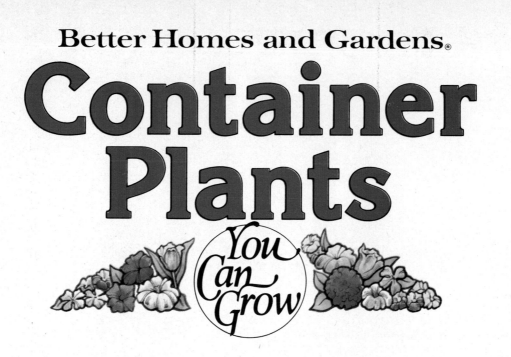

You Can Grow

© 1978 by Meredith Corporation, Des Moines, Iowa. All Rights Reserved.
Printed in the United States of America. First Edition. First Printing
Library of Congress Catalog Card Number: 78-56614
ISBN: 0-696-00375-9

CONTENTS

Gardening in Containers

Whatever good or ill may be said of man's dominion over the earth, there is no mistaking the bare fact that underlying his shift from cave to castle is an abiding partnership with a wide variety of plants.

This quiet, unheralded marriage with leafy things is often an association spawned by raw necessity. Plants produced food, while some, in the case of herbs, offered valued remedies for a host of bodily ailments.

Spots for Pots

However, the almost universal courtyard garden of antiquity, filled with ornamental flowers and decorative shrubs, attests to a different kind of need. Somehow, the silent miracle of living plants promised a soothing antidote to the unnerving clamor of progress.

In short order, cities and towns sprouted. Roads, aqueducts, coliseums, and row houses displaced field and stream. The marriage appeared threatened. But no matter how metropolitan man became, plants were never far behind. In place of courtyard gardens and flower beds, came containers, pots, and window boxes. In ancient Rome, almost every roof sported a well-tended garden. Today, populations are denser than they have ever been, while cities sprawl in greater and greater circles. But our ancient connection with plants persists. The current interest in container gardening is alive, well, growing. Fortunately for the container grower, the plants'

needs are few—a spongy material where roots can gain a foothold, good drainage, nutrients, and a few moments of attention.

Even though you have to pay plants little mind, the joys of container gardening are numerous. You can practically paint your own landscape. Because pots and other containers are portable, you can arrange plantings to suit your particular living or work area.

It's easy to fit the soil and other conditions to the specific plants you want to grow. As a result, you can contain practically anything that appeals to your horticultural tastes with little extra effort and the right size pot.

Because plants and pots are small, you can transform the most unlikely of nooks and crannies into a paradise of color and texture. Containers can be suspended by rope or wire, attached to a wall or fence, placed along a railing, submerged in water, or built to fit a stairway.

Best of all, plants in pots and boxes tend to be healthier. Good ventilation and diversified plantings keep bug populations down, while, at the same time, luxuriant leaf growth makes weeds the exception rather than the rule with container gardening.

Patio Gardens

An unlandscaped patio can be as uninviting as a debtors' prison. But decorated with strategically placed container plants, its harsh, angular lines will dissolve into a sea of soft color and fascinating leaf patterns. Shrubs, flowering annuals, bulbs, and even small fruit trees are ideal candidates for your container garden. If your affections gravitate to more utilitarian plants, plan on a section devoted to vegetables. Tomatoes, eggplant, lettuce, chard, and onions all do well in containers. At the same time, their unique growth habits add special interest to the decor of the patio.

One of the most attractive advantages of containers is their mobility. But getting the most from your plantings requires something of a painter's eye. Large bulky containers and dense plants, if grouped together, can cause a disturbing sense of imbalance. Or taller trees can cast dense shade where sun is needed or obscure a view instead of screen a driveway. Remember to keep larger plants in the background and flowering varieties in a spot where the light is right. Almost all container plants should be turned occasionally to encourage symmetrical, not lopsided, growth.

A miniature kumquat tree provides pleasing background texture as well as mottled shade for geraniums and primroses.

Framed in a wide variety of flowering bulbs, this semi-shaded patio provides a perfect haven for plants and people.

Deck Gardens

At first glance, an apartment deck can appear hopelessly insulated from the rich, colorful scenery of mother earth. But with a little imagination and the right choice of plants, the deck offers advantages found nowhere else.

Remember, though, that more often than not, strong winds will present a problem. If plants are not properly weighted with adequate sand mixed with the soil or set out in heavy-duty containers, a mischievous breeze will knock them over, causing irreparable damage. Many plants, such as fuschias, cannot tolerate the drying effects of wind and will wither and die in no time when set in an unprotected breezy spot.

However, the ravages of wind can be easily blunted by building an attractive lath screen at the windward side of the deck. A two- or three-foot lath overhang will provide just the right amount of partial shade some plants thrive on. At the same time, a wood divider draped with decorative plants will effectively screen an unsightly view or act as a distinctive backdrop.

An added advantage of the deck lies in the spaced flooring; it offers plenty of ventilation. Drainage problems are also alleviated because excess water can drain off quickly and easily.

A painted lath screen provides an attractive backdrop for a wide variety of plants and also functions as a windbreak.

Decorative containers combined with a thoughtful mix of flowering plants integrate the deck with the outdoors.

Pool Gardens

Water, water everywhere is the key to container growing. But water doesn't always have to sink quietly into the soil, never to be seen again except when it dribbles out after saturating the roots.

An ornamental pool tucked into a shady corner can turn out to be a happy asset, not only to the terrace, but to the plants as well. Trailing or vine plants, cascading over the pool side, together with a rainbow selection of flowering annuals or hanging plants, can transform a neglected wall into a favorite resting place. As water evaporates, the immediate area will be cooled. And moisture-loving plants will respond favorably to the slightly higher humidity that is created.

Not all pools, however, need to be elaborately constructed, reflecting lakes in order to be attractive. Small, elevated pools can be easily fashioned from heavy-duty plastic film supported by a wooden frame. Or a discarded tub or other container can be cleverly tucked among shrubs and other potted plants. An inexpensive circulating pump can be installed to create a visually pleasing fountain effect.

A decorative fountain couched in green becomes the focal point of this well-designed outside living area.

This breezeway between house and garage overflows with leafy splendor, even though the area gets few hours of sun a day.

Vertical Gardens

Compared to those who can afford to scatter plants with wild abandon, container growers have to use their wits to get the most from less. For example, think of your outdoor space as having a vertical dimension as well as a horizontal one.

Try displaying plants one above the other on a wall, either in hanging baskets or placed attractively on shelves. Not only do you take advantage of the entire plant, but you dramatically increase your total growing room, as well.

Or try your hand at creating a green wall. Nothing but a perpendicular garden, its foundation is wire mesh, such as 2½-inch chicken wire, stapled to a simple, sturdy wooden frame of 1x2s.

The freestanding green wall should be at least ten to 12 inches thick, so both sides can be attractively planted. The attached unit should be six to eight inches wide. Fill the mesh with sphagnum peat moss, and plant seedlings fairly deep, facing slightly upward. Saturate the entire unit thoroughly when watering, and feed plants occasionally with a balanced fertilizer. Water regularly unless rainfall is sufficient.

A wooden wall dramatically holds pots of ivy, geranium, and spider plant.

Easy-to-build shelves can transform a stark corner into a forest of brilliant flowers and delicate foliage.

Step Gardens

Steps either go up or down. Sometimes, when things get tricky, they twist mischievously around a corner or spiral through a hole in the ceiling. But by and large, stairs represent the lesser of a number of architectural evils. Their main purpose is almost entirely functional; that is, they get you from one level to another. The trouble is, they have the blocky, clumsy appearance that's unfortunately characteristic of a great many functional things.

Enter container plants. Any stairway, no matter how bleak, can become a unique garden paradise almost overnight with just a handful of container plants. If you pine for an avalanche of cascading color, choose the showy annuals, such as the dependable petunia, the carefree marigold, the brilliant zinnia, the riotous nasturtium, or the irrepressible calendula.

If time for gardening is scarce, consider the host of attractive perennials that do especially well in containers, because winter protection is effortless. Chrysanthemums and lilies are just some of the possibilities. For something a little more unusual, try a container or two of exotic ornamental grasses, such as cord grass, fountain grass, or clumps of blue fescue. Annual quaking grass grows from seed.

The brilliant, fluffy plumes of celosia Red Fox effectively soften the normally harsh lines of these stone steps.

Dwarf Cherry Buttons zinnia offers a seemingly unending profusion of color.

Showy flowers are made all the more attractive when combined with the subtle green of vines and other trailing plants.

Supplementing Other Plants

Moderation in all things, say the ancient philosophers. The same can be said for choosing ornamental plants. A patio awash in a monochromatic sea of a single variety can reduce a walkway or deck to a dull eyesore. If you become as familiar as possible with the range of available horticultural colors, leaf textures, and plant shapes (including height, number of stems, density, width, and growth habit), your container plantings will become a source of constantly changing visual delight.

Some plants, though, are natural companions. Petunias, white or purple, mingled with taller geraniums, offer pleasantly contrasting colors. Or combine the majestic simplicity of clematis with the stately container-grown hydrangeas.

Sometimes, ground-hugging types, such as dwarf marigolds, can be effectively interplanted with taller varieties, such as daisies, cornflowers, or delphinium. But flowers aren't all there is to it. Some leaf colors, shapes, and textures are show stoppers by themselves. Consider the variegated forms of coleus or ivy, or the intriguing patterns of the zonal geraniums, as well as evergreen shrubs. Or grow beautifully patterned caladiums.

Clematis, with its jumbo blossoms on delicate vines, is a perfect companion plant for low-growing hydrangeas.

The double-blossomed Salmon Bouquet petunias transform an out-of-the-way stairway into a showcase of color.

Balcony Gardens

With high-rise apartment buildings dotting the urban skyline like rampant dandelions in a neglected lawn, balcony gardens are flourishing. Railings, benches, and sunny, cement corners are gradually blossoming into color-splashed sanctuaries of flowering vines, ornamental shrubs, and, in some cases, pint-sized salad gardens, replete with lettuce, cherry tomatoes, scallions, carrots, and radishes.

Gardening in the sky is basically no different than anywhere else. But there are a few factors unique to balcony growing worth taking into account before investing time and money in pots and plants. To begin with, there is the pesky wind. Most plants react badly to the drying ef-fects of a constant breeze. The problem is that cramped root systems simply can't keep up with the moisture that is rapidly transpiring from the leaves. So leaves dehydrate, turn brown, and eventually drop off, unless you pay close attention to watering and misting.

Sudden gusts of wind can knock a plant flat on its stem. The remedy is simple: weight containers with lots of crushed rock (which will also help drainage), provide ample amounts of sand when mixing soil, or anchor containers to railing or balcony floor. Sometimes, tying several containers together is all that is needed to provide stability. If all else fails, blunt the wind with a wood fence or lath screen.

Petunia, impatiens, and fern thrive in specially constructed containers.

Even the tiniest of balconies can offer a potpourri of garden delights including coleus, fern, wax begonia, and browallia.

Hot Sunny Areas

The sun is the very magic fellow that makes things grow. But each growing plant has its own peculiar requirements when it comes to how much sunlight it needs. Some need to bathe luxuriantly in direct sunlight all day, while others, forced for centuries to make do under a canopy of leaves from larger trees, vines, and shrubs, can thrive in just a touch of sun.

For container growers, the ins and outs of the sun boil down to a minor consideration: most containers are portable. Any plants that appear to be suffering from a low quota of sun can just be picked up and moved to another location. However, you'll save time and anxiety if you check out the plants beforehand and make a mental note of the light they need.

Eighteen-inch terra-cotta pots exposed to full sun provide ideal growing conditions for a host of flowering plants.

Where desert-like conditions prevail, try a pot of the uniquely formed succulents or rely on dependable pelargoniums.

In general, the more profuse the blooms, the greater the amount of sunshine needed. But that doesn't mean a terrace or deck under a half-day's shade will never be graced with blossoms. Many plants do well in partial or mottled shade (see "Shady Areas," page 22).

Chances are, though, there will be one hot spot on the balcony, deck, or terrace that just can't seem to get out from under the sun. Naturally, things will get on the warm side, perfect for sun-loving, brightly tufted geraniums. Or choose among the marvelous selection of roses, some with climbing habit, others low growing. Then there is the vast array of flowering shrubs. Or you can play a kind of musical pots and use the sunny area for occasional plant therapy. When something needs a shot of sun, simply move containers around. At the same time, plants that have exhausted their flowering repertoire, can be moved out of the limelight to replenish themselves in an out-of-the-way spot.

However, sun and heat can play some mean tricks. Without ventilation and adequate watering, the sun spot can turn into a micro-desert that will dry up the hardiest of plants. Be sure containers are placed on blocks or pieces of wood to aid air circulation. Remember, too, that moisture loss will be greater in full sun than shade. Check the surface of the soil frequently, and water when it feels dry to the touch. In midsummer, when hot days are the rule, daily waterings may be necessary.

21

Shady Areas

Every day the sun silently etches a benevolent arc across the sky. Whether or not it penetrates the maze of walls, fences, and high-rise buildings that surround us is often left to chance. But, fortunately for the dedicated gardener, there are more growing things under the sun than are dreamed of in all our gardening schemes. Many of them thrive in shade.

If shade has claimed your outdoor living area, determine just where the darkest areas are. Remember that there are degrees of shade. Obstructions, like thick brick walls, cast a dense, almost hopeless, shade. But a stucco wall painted white and exposed to the sun will give off considerable reflected light. A portable wall that adjusts to the sun's angle can also help.

Mottled shade is not only a happy compromise between glaring sun and cavernous shade, but is ideal for many plants.

A welcome retreat from a scorching sun, this garden deck overflows with lush, shade-loving ferns, ivies, and evergreens.

Many trees and shrubs, on the other hand, cast a delightfully restful, mottled shade just right for such sun-sensitive plants as fuchsia, coleus, impatiens, or tuberous begonias. Where deep shade prevails, use the delicate fronds of the various ferns and the trailing vines of the ivies. Keep in mind, though, that all plants need light (as opposed to direct sun) to trigger the all-important, food-producing process called photosynthesis.

If flowers aren't the end-all of your gardening plans, all the better, because many plants are as remarkable for the quality of their foliage as others are for their blossoms. Consider, for example, the intriguing, scale-like structure of the junipers or arborvitae. Then there is the holly family, with a seemingly endless variety of attractively shaped leaves. Hollies are available as both deciduous or evergreen shrubs. Or you can revel among the fine-needled evergreens, such as mugho pine, hemlock, or black pine. Excellent for hedging,

evergreens can transform a dark, neglected corner into a cool, forest retreat. At the same time, there is an abundance of shrubs that will tolerate partial shade. Some are outstanding for the color and pattern of their leaves or stems, while others offer pleasing shapes. Still others add an unusually colorful note with brightly colored berries (see "Trees and Shrubs," page 48). Whatever your situation, the ideal plant is waiting somewhere in a nursery or catalog to brighten your shady area.

Water Gardens

All too often, water, the elixir of growing things, is relegated to the dark recesses of the soil where it seeps and gurgles out of view. But for centuries, water has been the plaything of gardeners. Medieval designers carved large moats around ornamental plantings, and the Japanese perfected the art of integrating small patches of water into outdoor gardens.

The Romans experimented earlier by tinkering with spigots and spouts to create delicately splashing fountains. For the modern gardener, the variations are practically infinite. Moving water can either gurgle softly, burble and splash with playful abandon, tumble in cascades, or simply sit still and reflect the surroundings with the silent perfection of clear glass.

The first step is to survey the terrace or backyard carefully in order to determine the best location for a water garden. You may want to enhance the beauty of a flowering tree or shrub by offering a reflected view of breathtaking flowers or interesting branch structure. Or you may want to enlist the soothing splash of falling water to mask disagreeable street noises. Often a small pool can show off a brilliant patch of flowering annuals. Devoting the pool to a selection of water plants is still another approach.

The main thing is to create a pleasing landscape in which plants, pool, and furniture naturally complement each other. Avoid placing the pool in the geometric center of things, so it looks more like a casual addition to the soothing setting.

Scale, too, is important. A pool too small or too large will seem out of joint and either dominate the scenery or become lost beneath a canopy of plants. If you have doubts, simply construct a mock-up from scrap wood and plastic film. Shift the model from one location to the other until you find the right combination.

Once the pool is in place, choose leisurely among the dramatic shapes and colors aquatic plants offer. Water lilies have unsurpassed beauty. Tropical varieties, however, have larger and more spectacular blooms than their hardier counterparts. Water lilies dislike running water; they resent disturbance or being splashed or rocked about. Use them in reflecting ponds or quiet pools instead of in merrily splashing fountains or waterfalls. Lilies are planted early in the spring, as soon as the water has warmed. Fill pool with water at least a week before planting. Then place lily rhizome in a five-inch pot (a plastic container will hold up better than a clay one) filled with ordinary garden soil. Cover with an inch of sand to keep soil particles in place. Then submerge the pot so the rim is anywhere from six to eight inches below water level. Place boards or stones under the pot in order to bring the rim to the desired height. Oxygenating grasses combined with fish and snails not only add to the exotic flavor, but also serve to keep water clean and algae at a minimum.

Other water plants provide fascinating displays of leaf texture, shape, and pattern. Ludwigia produces thin, wafer-like leaves that display a muted red color when exposed to the sun. Primose creeper (*Jussiaea repens*) offers light green leaves and attractive primrose-shaped blossoms. The water milfoils (*Myriophyllum verticillatum* or *M. aquaticum*) send sprays of exquisitely formed foliage above the surface of the water. A popular grass plant is eel grass (*Vallisneria spiralis*), with its translucent narrow leaves that sway, ghost-like, under water. A favorite among aquarium keepers, eel grass needs little maintenance. Whatever your choice, try to arrange the setting so the aquatic plants get at least six hours of full sun per day.

With plastic permeating every aspect of our technological lives, building a pool is an uncomplicated affair. Easy-to-install plastic pipe, submersible pumps, various spigots, valves, and couplers all make the business of circulating or squirting water within the mechanical abilities of most do-it-yourselfers. Most pumps simply consist of an intake and outlet valve, a three-wire electric cable (which must be properly grounded), a plastic hose, and a spray head designed for a fountain. Use an attractive arrangement of container plants to hide any unsightly pipes or other fittings.

As for the pool itself, anything that will hold water will do. Even a discarded washtub will serve the purpose. If water plants are to be the main attractions, then engineering a circulating pool is not absolutely necessary. Keep in mind, however, the water may have to be changed occasionally. An effective pool can be constructed easily from a wooden frame lined with heavy-duty plastic film. Or if you feel especially creative, sculpt your own pool by pouring concrete into a newly designed form.

A large, decorative planter filled with water offers a perfect setting for the spectacular blossoms of water lilies.

Window Boxes

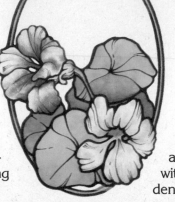

Windows for most people are for looking in or looking out. But to a designer of homes, a window is a small masterpiece of glass and trim that saves a wall from becoming acres of blank monotony. To the serious gardener who views plants as adjuncts to good living, as well as a fascinating pastime, windows represent a perfect excuse for growing things in containers.

The range of plants that can be cultivated successfully in the window container is much wider than most people realize. Even the summer-blossoming bulbs are possible with removable tray inserts, so the bulbs can be stored over winter. Window box holdings can range from an enchanted rose garden filled with miniatures to a tasty herb garden off the kitchen.

Easy to construct, a simple shelf with potted geraniums transforms an ordinary window into a dazzling floral display.

A window box coupled with two attractive containers offers a sun-splashed home for a variety of ornamental plants.

When planting an ornamental window garden, combine plants that nicely complement each other. For example, try combining the compact, erect-growing geranium or impatiens with the floppy trailing types, such as the ivies, browallia, or nasturtium. Remember, too, that a container packed with blossoming varieties might get a little gaudy if not tempered with something that offers more in the way of attractive foliage.

The window box can be constructed easily in a few hours, using scrap lumber or new wood purchased at a lumberyard. If you plan to paint the box to match window trim, use exterior plywood treated to withstand weathering. Remember, the thicker the wood, the greater its insulating power. The heavy-duty box will better protect the soil from variable temperatures. For most plants, a box eight to ten inches wide and at least eight inches deep will be satisfactory. The length will depend on the width of your window. For drainage, drill regularly spaced holes at least one-half inch in diameter in the bottom. Mount the box with steel shelf brackets. The short leg should be nearly the width of the box. Always mount the brackets with the long leg against the wall.

For soil, use any lightweight potting soil, or mix your own, using equal parts garden loam, peat moss, and perlite. Cover the bottom of the box with broken clay pot fragments, and add a layer of coarse peat moss or nylon netting. Then fill with soil. A handful of slow-release fertilizer thoroughly mixed with the soil will help keep plants healthy. Moisten the soil thoroughly and set out plants. Once the plants begin to bloom, be sure to pinch off faded flowers. If the plants are allowed to go to seed, they will stop blooming. Well-cared-for plants will reward you with lush, healthy growth and a bonus of unending blossoms.

Use exterior plywood or treated planks for containers. Holes allow drainage.

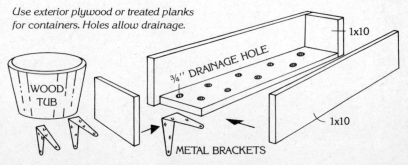

Hanging Baskets

Give a plant, any plant, a respectable dose of light, air, moisture, and soil, and the chances are it will grow anywhere—dangling from a ceiling, perched on a swinging shelf, or cascading from a wire basket. If a deck or patio appears on the drab side, a decorative plant can enliven things with a simple turn of a screw or hook. Or wispy, trailing plants can soften the massive structural lines of a porch or stairway. Windows and doorways lose some of their bland geometry when adorned with brightly colored basket plants. For the terrace gardener, whose horticultural ambitions have to be kept in continual check, the hanging garden adds a new dimension. Up and out of the way, plants in mid air are out from under foot.

A hanging basket overflowing with allyssum, fibrous begonia, and viola adds an eye-catching splash of color.

1 All you need to get your hanging garden under way is a wire basket, some sphagnum peat moss, a bag of ordinary potting soil, and several flats of healthy seedlings. For starters, try alyssum, wax begonias, or pansies. First soak the peat moss in a bucket of water (overnight, if possible), and then drain off the water and shape the moss into flattened cakes. If necessary, gently squeeze out excess water.

2 Line the basket by working the peat moss around the inside and between the wires. Simply squeeze moss between wires and allow them to spring back. Continue adding moss until the lining is at least 1½ inches thick. Then check carefully for thin spots where soil may filter through. Add moss, if necessary. To create a consistent lining, try to work the fibers together as you work the moss into flat cakes.

3 Complete the basket by placing a cushion of moss around the wire rim. Slowly fill the resulting cavity with potting soil. To distribute soil evenly, jiggle the basket from side to side so soil fills the basket completely. Once the basket is full, settle the soil by gently tapping the bottom of the basket on a tabletop. Soil should be packed just firmly enough to force the peat moss lining snugly against the outside wire.

4 Lay basket on its side and insert seedlings into the soil through the moss lining. Use your fingers or a dibble to poke planting holes into the basket. Be sure roots are covered with soil. For a foliage ball effect, plant an erect-growing plant (geranium, for instance) in the center of the top opening. When planting is complete, suspend the basket on a decorative chain and water generously.

PLANTS THAT HANG WELL

What you grow in your elevated garden depends on whether your plans call for selected splashes of color or the quiet, unobtrusive beauty of subtly tinted leaves. Remember, though, careless mixing of too many colors can create an overwhelming billboard effect that will jangle the nerves, rather than inspire repose. The best approach is to mix judiciously the qualities of both foliage and flowering types.

FLOWERING PLANTS

AZALEA When someone mentions azaleas, most people think of vast landscaped lawns. But there are hybrid varieties available that produce the same outstanding blossoms when grown in a hanging container. Just like its larger counterpart, however, these compact azaleas also need acid soil. Use equal parts of peat moss and a general potting soil for the best results. It prefers diffused light and soil that is kept slightly moist. When applying fertilizer, use plant food designed especially for acid-loving plants.

BEGONIA (pendulous and wax types) Hardly surpassed for their beauty, the pendulous begonias are a natural for the hanging garden. Happier in partial shade with temperatures on the cool side, begonias like a humus soil that is allowed to dry out a bit between waterings. The pendulous begonias are tuberous. When you water less frequently as the leaves die back, the tubers can be lifted and stored in a cool, dark place, then replanted outdoors the next summer.

IVY GERANIUM Geranium lovers need not despair when their gardening centers around hanging baskets. The ivy geranium combines the grace of the trailing ivy with the unmatched blossoms of geraniums. Well-drained soil and full sun are essential. Soil should be allowed to dry between waterings. Pinch back to encourage bushy growth.

LOBELIA (Trailing) Lush and lacy, lobelia could qualify as the queen of hanging plants because of its deli-

Hanging Baskets

cate blue flowers that bloom the entire summer. Ideal for partial shade or northern exposure, it likes moist, but not wet, soil.

PETUNIA No list would be complete without the spectacular, and equally popular, trumpet blossoms of petunia. An easy-to-grow annual, petunias need full sun and an average soil that allows good drainage.

FOLIAGE PLANTS

BEGONIA For a fascinating variation in color and shape, few plants can match the fancy-leaved begonias. The best known, rex begonia, has large multicolored foliage, while fern begonia produces fernlike stems. Most like diffused bright light, adequate humidity, and moist soil.

FERN Boston, maidenhair, and asparagus are just a handful of those available. All do better in partial shade or indirect light and moist soil. Their gracefully drooping fronds are excellent as background foliage for other plants.

IVY Although they're often attacked by mites, the ivies are just too handsome to ignore because of an insect or two. German ivy is fast growing with tender leaves and stems, while English ivy is tough enough to survive northern winters. Needlepoint ivy is especially attractive because of its slender, pointed leaves and long, branching stems. Most do best in partial shade. English ivy can't stand direct sun.

PEPEROMIA A staple among container enthusiasts, the shiny, waxy leaves on trailing branches offer a lustrous note of color that also stands out in any suspended garden. Keep plants in indirect sun or mottled shade, and maintain soil moisture to prevent drying out.

CARE AND MAINTENANCE

While suspended baskets add an unusual dimension to gardening, they may need a little extra attention when it comes to care and feeding. A container dangling in mid air is neither here nor there in relation to the good earth where most living things make their home. As a result, hanging plants are more exposed to the elements than their grounded counterparts. Soil dries out much faster, and leaves, constantly tossed about by the wind, lose moisture at a frightening rate. Also, temperature differences between the floor and the porch ceiling can vary as much as ten degrees Fahrenheit. A cool day for a floor plant could be a scorcher for something a mere six feet higher.

Prevent drying out by keeping a close watch on the level of soil moisture. During summer months, waterings should be at least once a day; during hot spells, additional waterings may be called for. Once plants launch new growth, be sure regular feedings are given at weekly intervals.

Verbena, with its trailing habit and soft shades of lavender, pink, and white, is an ideal choice for an airborne container.

31

Strawberry Jars

Few things are in greater need of a better name than the strawberry jar, because it is neither restricted to strawberry growing alone, nor is it small enough to be properly called a jar. When it comes to mixing plants and pots, however, this jar, which is really a jug, offers many inspiring possibilities. You can grow anything from beans to begonias. Think of trailing or semi-trailing plants, though, when choosing varieties for your strawberry jar. Flowering browallia, alyssum, lobelia, petunia, and violets are all good candidates. For an intriguing display of finely formed and subtly tinted foliage, look to the array of trailing, non-flowering plants available, such as the ivies, the fancy-leaved begonias, and, of course, the ferns. If growing your own food strikes you as the economical thing to do, use your strawberry jar for a vertical herb garden. A large jar can support a cherry tomato or two plus a cucumber, melon, or a squash vine. And then, naturally, there is the exquisite strawberry, which not only offers unusual leaf shapes interspersed with snow white blossoms, but also produces delicious fruit. With good soil, proper planting, a protected location, and conscientious watering, all will thrive handsomely in your garden.

1 Before filling the strawberry jar with soil, first place a layer of broken crockery or gravel in the bottom to ensure proper drainage. The larger the jar, the deeper the layer of drainage material should be. Top layer of crockery or stones with a second layer of coarse peat moss or wire mesh (old window screening will do), so soil won't filter down into the drainage material. A jar more than two feet in height ought to have a cylinder of wire mesh inserted down the center so deep watering is possible. Then add soil.

2 After the jar is filled, including all the pockets, insert two or three seedlings into the soil in each opening. Start from the bottom, and work your way up so seedlings already planted are not damaged. For large containers and plants with fairly extensive root systems, insert plants as you fill the jar with soil. Simply fill bottom of jar with drainage material, and add soil up to bottom of lowest level pockets. Spread out roots of seedlings, and cover completely with soil up to next level. Proceed up the jar, filling and planting each level.

3 For the final step, fill top opening with seedlings and water completely. For instant color, plant well-established seedlings purchased at a garden supply center or nursery. Most will already be in flower or at least covered with swelling buds. Or start seeds indoors well before the growing season starts. If you have the time and patience, you can always start seed directly in the pockets. But once plants have emerged and are established, be sure to give the jar a quarter turn each day so plants get equal sun.

A strawberry jar filled with rich, moist soil can be striking when planted with profusely flowering plants.

ABCs of Annuals

Whether you're a veteran gardener or just a novice, you can add bright spots of color to your yard almost overnight with annual flowers. Most grow quickly from seed, require little maintenance, and flower from early spring right up until frost. Annual flowers also take kindly to container culture and make ideal floral accents for patios, decks, balconies, and porches. A quick change of containers can alter the mood or emphasis of any outdoor living area. Many plants can even be brought indoors during the winter for an extra show of color.

Petunias, pansies, and geraniums grow easily in large clay containers.

THE VERSATILITY OF ANNUALS

Beauty without bother. That's the goal you'll be able to achieve when you garden with annual flowers. They'll bloom reliably all summer long and require only routine care in exchange. Plus, they are available in such a variety of forms and colors they lend themselves to almost any planting situation. You can find squat, thick, tall, thin, petite, and feathery forms with a nearly endless variety of color.

GETTING STARTED Although it's probably less expensive to start annuals from seed, you'll get a lot for your investment in started seedlings.

For one thing, you'll be rewarded with at least one extra month of color. And for another, your started seedlings will be able to withstand midsummer heat better than slower seed-started plants can.

Each spring, most nurseries and garden supply houses stock a wide, and often confusing, selection of started annual varieties. To be sure you get what your planting scheme calls for, read the plant label before buying. It will tell you the variety name, blossom color, and future height of your seedlings. Always pick short, stocky plants with a healthy appearance and bright green color.

SOIL Before planting any young annual seedlings, have plenty of porous potting soil on hand. Planted directly into the ground, most annuals will be able to thrive, even if the soil is poor. But grown in pots, where ordinary garden soil has a tendency to dry out and compact, annuals will not prosper.

Most commercial potting soil mixes are more than adequate for ordinary annual flower culture. But if you need a large amount of soil, you might want to try mixing your own, using equal parts of garden soil, sand, peat moss, and perlite or vermiculite.

PLANTING Before potting up your seedlings, remove them from their plastic growing containers. To do this, grasp the base of the plants with one hand and turn the container upside down. Most of the time, the plants will just slip out, but if you have trouble, tap the bottom of the container with a trowel.

Then, after you've knocked the plants out, gently separate them so they can be planted at the proper intervals. Use a sharp knife and cut around each plant, slowly pulling and working the roots free. Keep the soil moist at all times so it won't fall away from the roots.

To plant your seedlings, dig a hole slightly larger than the root ball of the plant. If the roots of the plant are tightly compacted, gently loosen them and place them in the hole. Clip away any excessively long or trailing roots. When the plant is in place, fill in around it with soil, and water heavily to eliminate air pockets around the roots.

SPACING AND CARE When grown in pots or raised beds, most annuals will look more attractive when they are planted close together. Space low, edging plants, like sweet alyssum, lobelia, and dwarf marigolds, about three to five inches apart, taller plants, like petunias, celosia, and coleus, about four to six inches apart.

After planting, always try for good foliage and bushy plant forms. The abundant show of flowers will follow naturally. Keep the blooms coming by proper watering whenever rainfall is not enough. And cut out all faded flowers as they appear to keep them from going to seed. This will result in the development of a new crop of flowers. Also, keep varieties of annuals that have a tendency to get leggy, like petunias and coleus, pinched back to encourage a bushy, compact growth habit.

WINDOW BOXES A two-way pleasure, a window box is a great way to improve your outlook and to share your flowering annuals with neighbors. With the aid of shelf brackets, window boxes are a snap to install.

For the non-window box astride the balcony railing, build a "saddlebag" planter by joining two boxes to fit over the rail. If you like, mount a third box for the saddle bridge to straddle the rail.

Arrange your plants first for the indoor view, and then for the outsiders looking in. If privacy is your aim, add climbing or tall plants to the arrangement.

Keep an eye out for signs of too much midday heat, wind damage, or too much shade. Shift plants around to their individual likings. So long as they are kept within reach of a watering can, you're bound to succeed.

If your window box gets little sun, use shade-loving plants. Wax begonias or impatiens will keep the area colorful.

FALL CARE Another one of the beauties of gardening with annuals is that many can easily be propagated in the late summer and potted up as colorful winter houseplants. Coleus, impatiens, and geraniums are the easiest plants to grow from cuttings.

Take cuttings from strong, healthy stems, making the cut about six inches down on the stem, and trim off the bottom leaves. You can dip the cuttings in a rooting hormone to make the rooting process faster, but most cuttings will do almost as well without it.

Then insert the cuttings in moistened vermiculite. (They can also be rooted in water, but the roots will tend to be more brittle.) If you're rooting many cuttings, you may want to use a flat pan or dish. Place your cuttings in indirect light, and in several weeks they should be well rooted.

When plants have roots about two inches in length, transfer them to individual two- or three-inch pots. Pot with a good potting soil and water thoroughly. Place the plants in indirect light for a week or two, and then transfer them to their permanent locations in the house.

MIXING AND MASSING Container gardening with annuals is particularly useful where garden plots are small, because it encourages multiple use of terrace space for both plants and people. In addition, you can rearrange containers to change the emphasis, alter the mood, or bring plants into the spotlight as they come into peak bloom.

If space is really limited, hang baskets of colorful annuals from the

ceiling, or set small pots of tiny plants on a porch railing. And use window boxes on a ledge or sill for suspended pockets of coleus, geraniums, or begonias.

With the wide variety of annuals available, it's easy to develop a personal style for your garden. For a bright informal look, mix pots of different colored annuals together. In larger boxes and beds, the different varieties can be planted together.

Some good flowering and foliage combinations to try include: Blue Blazer ageratum with Carpet of Snow alyssum, white candytuft with purple lobelia, white petunias with red or orange nasturtiums, deep blue petunias with red verbena, coleus with Rocket snapdragons, dwarf yellow marigolds with pansies, or Jewel Box celosia with Sprinter geraniums. And for the quieter backdrops, don't overlook the foliage plants. Dusty miller, coleus, and flowering kale can make a handsome foil for brilliant dwarf zinnias or marigolds.

For a more formal look with strong impact, use a mass planting of one kind of flower or a subtle blending of near colors of the same plant. Mass plantings also make for easier care.

For sunny spots, cluster pots of Blue Blazer ageratum, dwarf calliopsis, dwarf double calendula, Jewel Box celosia, Magic Charms dianthus, Sprinter or standard geraniums, lobelia, dwarf marigolds, nasturtiums, pansies, petunias, Floral Carpet snapdragons, and dwarf or Mexican zinnias. For slightly shady spots, use coleus, impatiens, or fibrous begonias.

If you want tall back-up color, pot up Topper snapdragons, Bright Lights cosmos, or linaria seedlings, and place them in a location sheltered from high winds. Or grow one or more hybrid morning glories or cathedral bells from seed in a pot fitted with bamboo trellising.

CHOOSING THE RIGHT VARIETY It's important to know the colors, heights, preferred environment, and special culture of each species you intend to grow before you plant. On the next four pages you'll find in easy-to-locate alphabetical order a quick rundown of annual flowers that grow well in containers.

ANNUAL SELECTION

AGERATUM (flossflower) Plants grow 8 to 12 inches tall, producing small fuzzy blooms in shades of blue or violet. There are also white-and pink-flowering varieties. Ageratum grows easily in full sun or partial shade but does require a steady supply of moisture for greatest growth. You can start plants eight to ten weeks early indoors, but seedlings grow slowly and are rather tender. You may prefer to buy started transplants for best results. Keep faded flowers pinched to encourage continuous bloom. Compact shape makes it an excellent border plant. Good varieties include: Blue Blazer, Blue Mink, Midget Blue, and Summer Snow.

ALYSSUM, SWEET These low-growing, fragrant plants rarely get over 4 inches tall but with good care will carpet an area 8 to 9 inches in diameter. Plants are tolerant of hot, dry conditions and are perfect added to hanging baskets, window boxes, or tucked in around the base of taller plants. White, rose, and violet are the three most common colors. Start plants indoors from seeds 8 to 10 weeks before the last expected frost or buy started transplants. If flowering decreases toward the end of the summer, trim plants back to encourage new growth. In the fall, bring well-grown specimens indoors as a winter houseplant. Good varieties include: Carpet of Snow, Rosie O'Day, Royal Carpet, and Violet Queen. In the South, plants will often bloom all year long.

ANCHUSA (summer forget-me-not) Similar to true forget-me-nots, this annual features clusters of tiny five-petaled flowers on stiff, hairy stems, 1½ to 2 feet tall. Anchusa requires a rich, moist soil and a location that receives full sun. Start seeds indoors six to eight weeks before the last frost is due. Move seedlings to their permanent locations after the weather is reliably warm. To keep plants bushy and compact, cut plants back to about six inches after the first bloom fades. A good choice for window boxes and larger pots. Two popular varieties are Blue Angel and Blue Bird.

ASTER (callistephus) Aster varieties range in size from 8-inch dwarfs to 3-foot giants. Although all types can be grown in containers, you'll have better luck if you stick with the lower-growing varieties. Start seeds indoors about 6 weeks before the last expected frost. Seed-started plants will often not begin to bloom until mid-July. For earlier color, buy started transplants. Asters are available in an almost limitless array of colors, which include rose, white, yellow, pink, red, lavender, and salmon. Good varieties are Dwarf Queen, Pinocchio, Color Carpet, and Powderpuffs.

BALSAM Also known as garden balsam, touch-me-not, and lady slipper, balsam is a close relative of the common impatiens. Bush forms that grow only 10 inches tall are recommended for container gardening and produce camellia-like pink, red, salmon, purple, or white flowers at the tops of the plants.

Balsams do best in rich, well-drained soil that is kept slightly moist and receives full sun. Sow seeds indoors 4 to 6 weeks before the last expected frost, or buy started transplants. Popular dwarf varieties include Tom Thumb and Double Flowered Dwarf. Take cuttings in late summer for overwintering indoors.

BEGONIA (wax begonia or fibrous begonia) Sporting attractive foliage as well as eyecatching flowers, begonias quickly form compact 6- to 9-inch plants. The clusters of flowers can be either single or double, depending on the variety, and are usually available in shades of red, pink, and white. Foliage ranges from bright green to a reddish-bronze. Begonias will grow under almost any light conditions, so long as they are kept well watered. They are especially useful for shady garden corners. Start from seed 4 to 6 months early indoors, or buy transplants. Occasionally pinch back plants to promote compact growth. In late summer, take cuttings for wintertime color. Popular varieties include: Vodka, Gin, Whisky, Linda, Thousand Wonders White, and Thousand Wonders Rose.

BROWALLIA These compact, sprawling plants quickly reach 10 inches in height and may cover a 10- to 15-square-inch area. Flowers are petunia-like and appear right up until

The colorful foliage of the coleus makes it a must for the shady garden.

frost. The most commonly available colors are blue, violet, or white, Browallia can be grown in either full sun or partial shade but do require a moist, rich soil. Sow seeds indoors 8 to 10 weeks before the last expected frost. Or buy nursery transplants. To keep the plants compact, pinch back any shoots that start to get leggy. Browallia is a good choice for hanging baskets and window boxes. They may be cut back in the fall and potted for indoor winter blooms. Three popular varieties are Blue Bells Improved, Silver Bells, or Velvet Blue.

CANDYTUFT (iberis) Although candytuft is available in both dwarf and standard forms, the dwarf varieties are by far the most useful in container gardens. These hardy 6- to 13-inch plants produce flat-topped clusters of rose, pink, crimson, lavender, or white flowers. They grow in full sun or partial shade, although in exceptionally hot areas they do have a tendency to burn out. Sow seed in the early spring outdoors, and transplant the seedlings to pots as soon as their second true set of leaves appears.

Candytuft will thrive in almost any soil type. After the first flowering, trim back the plants to stimulate a second bloom. To ensure color all summer long, make several sowings in the spring at two-to three-week intervals. Umbellata Dwarf Fairy is a popular variety. Cut flowers make fine fresh bouquets.

CASTOR BEAN (ricinus) Primarily grown as an exotic foliage plant, these quick-growing plants usually reach 10 feet or more. Each palmlike leaf may be 1 to 3 feet in length. Because of their large size, castor beans are generally planted directly in the garden or in large tubs. For good growth, castor beans need full sun and plenty of heat and moisture. Start seeds indoors 6 to 8 weeks before the last frost, or wait to sow outdoors after the weather has warmed. In mild climates, plants may last several years. Flowers are inconspicuous, and seed pods are poisonous and should be clipped before they mature, especially if children are likely to be in the area. Also, some people are allergic to both the seed pods and the foliage.

The drought-resistant dwarf marigold thrives even in a small amount of soil.

CELOSIA or COCKSCOMB
Cockscomb (crested) and plumosa (feathered) are the common names for the two most common celosias. Both names describe the shape of the brilliantly colored flowers that appear in red, yellow, orange, and pink. Dwarf forms average about 8 inches in height, while taller varieties may reach 18 to 24 inches. Both types of celosia require full sun but can tolerate most any kind of soil. Start seeds 6 to 8 weeks early indoors, or buy nursery transplants. Always use celosia with discretion, because their bright colors will often overpower other flowers. Flower heads make excellent additions to dried flower arrangements. Cut flowers before black, bead-like seeds appear. Hang bunches upside down in a dry, well-ventilated area. Popular varieties include: Jewel Box, Lilliput, Empress, Gladiator, Red Fox, and Crusader.

COLEUS Colorful foliage and quick growth are the trademarks of this popular annual. Leaf colors include: yellow, pink, white, red, and green in endless combinations. As the plants mature, they also produce either white or blue flower spikes. Plants range from 6 inches to 24 inches tall and should be kept pinched to encourage compact growth.

Coleus grows best in a rich, moist soil where they are protected from direct sunlight. Start new plants from seeds sown indoors in midwinter, or buy nursery transplants. In late summer, take stem cuttings and pot up as winter houseplants.

COSMOS These tall, graceful plants have finely cut foliage and 3- to 4-inch daisy-like flowers in shades of pink, rose, yellow, red, or lavender. Mature plants will often reach 6 feet tall. Because of their height, cosmos are best utilized in large planting boxes or tubs. Plant cosmos in a sunny location. Staking may be necessary, especially in windy spots. They are extremely tolerant of poor, fairly dry soil. Start seeds directly outdoors after all danger of frost has passed.

Common single- and double-flowering varieties include Dazzler, Radiance, Sensation, and Bright Lights.

Magic Charms dianthus grows six inches high, every inch loaded with flowers.

DUSTY MILLER (centaurea) A good choice for hot, dry planting pockets, dusty miller almost seems to thrive on neglect. It's grown primarily for its attractive, silvery-white, fernlike foliage and will often reach 15 inches in height. Plants are slow to grow from seed, so purchase started seedlings from the nursery or garden center. Dusty Miller is an excellent choice for combination plantings with brightly colored or flowering annuals. They are especially desirable in window boxes and other hard-to-water locations.

GERANIUM (pelargonium) This versatile group includes nearly 600 different varieties. The most common colors are shades of red, pink, and white. Foliage may be green or variegated, large-leaved or small. Most commonly found are the zonals, with their bush-like structure; the trailing ivies; and the scenteds, whose leaves give off various

fragrances when rubbed. Start seeds 12 to 16 weeks before the last expected frost, or buy nursery transplants. Geraniums will grow almost anywhere but will put on their biggest show of color in full sun. Soil should be well drained and not too rich. Keep faded flowers clipped to encourage continuous bloom. In the fall, take stem cuttings for winter houseplants. Common standard varieties include Colorcade and Martha Washington. The new Sprinter varieties grow faster from seed and mature earlier than the standards.

IMPATIENS These compact, shade-loving plants—usually 6 to 18 inches tall—mound to cover a wide area. The flat blossoms resemble violets and appear all over the plant in shades of pink, red, purple, orange, white, and bicolors. Foliage on some varieties is variegated, with cream or yellow stripes. Start plants indoors 4

to 6 weeks before the last expected frost, or buy nursery transplants. Young seedlings are exceedingly cold tender, so be sure the weather is consistently warm before setting the plants outdoors. Keep plants pinched to encourage more compact growth. In late summer, take stem cuttings for wintertime houseplants. Reliable hybrid varieties include Elfin, Zig-Zag, and Imp.

LOBELIA (*Lobelia erinus*) These dainty, compact plants are also available in trailing varieties. Plants grow to 6 inches tall and are covered with ½-inch flowers. Blooms are usually blue, although they may be white, pink, or rose. Foliage can be either dark green or green bronze. Lobelia takes a long time to develop from seed and needs to be started at least 12 weeks early indoors. Or buy started transplants. Plant lobelia where it receives full sun in a rich, moist soil. If summers are excessively hot in your area, move potted lobelia away from strong sunlight. After first blossoms have faded, cut the plant back to encourage a second blooming. Depending on the variety, lobelia may be used in hanging baskets, window boxes, or as borders in large tubs. Move potted plants indoors in late summer to provide wintertime bloom. Two popular varieties are Bright Eyes and Crystal Palace.

MARIGOLD (tagetes) Often considered one of the easiest annuals to grow, marigolds are available in sizes ranging from 6-inch dwarfs to 3-foot standards. Flowers vary from bright orange to yellow, gold, and cream and white. Foliage is deep green and finely cut, with a pungent scent. Marigolds can tolerate almost any soil type as long as they receive full sun. Start seeds indoors 4 to 6 weeks early or directly outdoors after the danger of frost has passed. Started transplants are also commonly available at most greenhouses and nurseries. For container gardens, stick with the lower-growing forms: Goldie, King Tut, Bolero, and Gypsy. Naughty Marietta is a reliable single-flowered variety.

MORNING GLORY For tall backup

color, few annuals can beat the vining morning glory. Easily grown, these annual climbers quickly reach 8 feet in height. Start seeds 4 to 5 weeks early indoors, or sow the seeds directly outdoors and transplant seedlings to their containers when they have developed their second true set of leaves. Plant morning glory in a location that receives full sun. These all-day bloomers also work well trailing from window boxes and hanging baskets. Flower colors available include blue, scarlet, white, pink, and purple. Reliable varieties include: Heavenly Blue, Pearly Gates, Scarlett O'Hara, and Early Call.

PANSY Face-like markings on large, open flowers characterize this old-fashioned favorite. The overlapping petals of each flower combine variations of stripes and blotches in shades of purple, blue, yellow, dark rose, and white. Start seeds about 10 weeks before planting time or buy started transplants. Pansies need full sun but should be protected from hot dry weather. A rich, moist soil is a must. Pick back stems to encourage bushiness, and remove faded flowers as they appear. For extra-large flowers, allow only four or five flower stems per plant. Some of the best known varieties include cardinal-red Alpenglow, large-blossomed Moon Moth, multi-colored Paramount, Coronation Gold, and heat-resistant Imperial Blue.

PETUNIA No other annual flower offers the variety in color or flower form as the petunia. One main type is classified as multiflora, indicating that it blooms freely, producing 2- to 3-inch single and double flowers on branching plants 12 to 15 inches high. A second type is classified as grandiflora. These plants also reach 15 inches in height but bear flowers that may reach 5 inches across in both single and double forms. Seeds are small and hard to start, so it's often easier to buy nursery transplants. Plant in full sun in rich, moist soil. Keep plants pinched back to encourage bushiness and remove faded flowers to encourage continuous blooms. They're perfect for borders, window boxes, hanging baskets, tubs, and planters. When

weather turns cool, transfer pots to a sunny window indoors. Good varieties to try are the trailing grandiflora Red Cascade; the hybrid grandifloras Malibu (blue), Happiness (pink), and Sunburst (yellow); and the multiflora hybrids Comanche (red) and Sugar Plum (lilac).

PINKS (dianthus) The common name of this annual refers to the fringed or pinked edges of the flower

petals. Pinks are available in red, white, and bicolors. Most will reach 12 inches in height with good care. Start seeds 7 weeks early indoors or directly outdoors after the danger of frost is over. For quicker bloom, buy started transplants. Keep plants trimmed to encourage continuous flower production and to discourage seed formation. Try scarlet red hybrid Queen of Hearts, white-edged China Doll, or early-flowering Magic Charms.

Colorful Richmondensis fibrous begonias hang above a box of bedding begonias.

39

ABCs of Bulbs

At first glance, a dried and shaggy bulb seems little more than a shriveled reminder of better days. Yet inside is a tiny plant, with all its parts waiting to spring to life as soon as the right elements are present. In a sense, a bulb is a horticultural time bomb with the potential for devastating beauty. But, bulbs are not strictly dormant. They continue to develop, even after flowers and leaves have long since vanished. While winter swirls in a wild fury overhead, bulbs are quietly storing food for the spring that is sure to follow.

The world of bulbs offers a wide variety of exquisitely formed blossoms.

For the container grower, bulb gardening offers unique rewards. To begin with, bulbs are the harbingers of spring, stealing the show long before other plants have recovered from the winter. At the same time, you can pull out a few choice varieties from the storage bin and force them into bloom for midwinter flowers. Daffodils, tulips, crocus, hyacinth, and galanthus can all be tricked into blooming before the spring solstice arrives. Or dabble in some of the show flowers, such as gladiolus, dahlias, or tuberous begonias.

The world of bulbs can be divided into two categories: those that survive winters for a spectacular spring show and those that must be

---

⟨❧ BLOOM SEQUENCE CHART ❧⟩

To get the most from your bulb bed, plant according to the sequence chart below. Blooms begin with the early galanthus (snowdrop) in March and end with lilies that fill July with color.

Galanthus (snowdrop)
Eranthis (winter aconite)
Crocus
Scilla, Siberian
Iris, reticulata and danfordiae
Chionodoxa (glory-of-snow)
Anemone blanda
Puschkinia
Tulip, botanical
Leucojum (snowflake)
Fritillaria

Daffodil, large cupped
Tulip, single and double early
Hyacinth
Daffodil, medium cupped
Tulip, triumph and Darwin hybrid
Daffodil, short cupped, jonquil
Tulip, parrot, cottage, lily
   flowered, peony flowered
Scilla, Spanish
Iris, Dutch
Lilies

dug in the fall after flowers and foliage have faded. The wise gardener, however, shouldn't worry about details when planning the container garden, so he or she can enjoy a wide variety of blooms, as well as a complete summer packed with color.

HOW TO GROW BULBS

Bulbs are among the easiest plants to grow. But to get the best bloom, keep these factors in mind:

1. Perhaps the most important element in good bulb culture is good drainage. If the soil is too wet, bulbs may rot and succumb to disease.

2. Although a bulb contains a storehouse of plant nutrients, it can't go on indefinitely without some replenishment. Keep soil fertilized with bone meal, especially after the first flowering season. Work in material so nutrients penetrate to where roots can absorb them.

3. Proper planting depth is crucial to healthy and extensive root development. As a general rule, plant a bulb to a depth equal to 2½ to three times its diameter. Smaller bulbs may be planted slightly deeper.

Because they are continually working, try to get bulbs into the soil as soon as possible after you buy them. Hardy bulbs in particular need to be planted in the fall to be triggered by cold winter temperatures. If temporary storage is unavoidable, place bulbs in a cool, dry place until ready to plant. Tender bulbs, like tuberous begonias, are generally started indoors in February or March, then transplanted to containers in time for spring bloom.

Just because blooms have opened and illuminated the patio with glorious color doesn't mean the show is over for bulbs. As soon as petals begin to fade, the bulb prepares for the next season's growth. Leaves continue to manufacture food, which then is transferred to the bulb's subterranean storehouse. If other flowers are slated for deck or patio, simply move the bulb containers to one side where the plants can carry on their silent preparations. This is a good time to make the rounds of your bulb tubs, snapping off blossom heads so plants will not exhaust

themselves forming useless seed pods. Also, apply a sprinkling of fertilizer to help the bulb recoup some of its losses. Only when the leaves begin to droop and turn brown should you think about lifting bulbs.

When purchasing bulbs, keep a sharp eye out for quality. Examine it carefully for cracks and evidence of disease or rotting. Large bulbs are expensive and better used at exhibitions. Small bulbs may be inexpensive, but blooms will be sparse if at all. The best bet is a medium-size bulb that feels firm and hefty.

SOME POPULAR BULBS

ANEMONE Hardy. Often called windflower, anemone offers a wide range of deep colors, with blossoms on short stems or long stems. Some bear single, poppy-like flowers, while others have attractive double blossoms. Anemones need a well-drained soil for proper bulb growth and development. When preparing your container mix, be sure to include ample amounts of coarse sand. If weight is a consideration, use perlite. Although

fairly hardy, plants should be located in partial shade and protected with a mulch to preserve soil moisture. Be sure soil is well supplied with nutrient-rich compost or other fertilizer. Set bulbs out about six inches apart and about three or four inches deep. Some gardeners like to stagger plantings to enjoy continuous bloom. Poppy anemones can remain in the ground over winter, but in colder areas, lift and store blanda and apennine varieties for replanting next spring.

BEGONIA (tuberous) Tender. For richness of bloom and variety of color, the aspiring container gardener couldn't do better than concentrate on tuberous begonias. Easy to grow, begonias can be used to accent with color or to create a showy carpet of foliage bespeckled with luscious blossoms. Begonias do best in shade or partly shaded areas. They are so varied in growth habit, they often resemble other plants. Examples are the camellia flowered begonia, the carnation, narcissus, and the rose flowered variety. Pendulous begonias are perfect for hanging baskets.

By whatever name, the daffodil is unsurpassed for beauty of form and color.

For richness of blooms and foliage, try the ever-popular begonias.

CALADIUM Tender. For the deck gardener in the market for a dazzling foliage plant, the fancy-leaved caladiums will fit the bill. In combinations of green, white, pink, red, or silver, they make ideal companion plants for darker-leaved varieties. Or create a string of color by planting in long, narrow boxes placed end to end. In March, start tubers indoors in flats filled with sphagnum peat moss, and transplant as soon as all danger of frost has passed. Take care in transplanting because tender roots are injured easily. In fall, take up tubers, allow to dry out, and treat with an all-purpose garden dust before storing. Place in dry vermiculite at 50 degrees.

CANNA Tender. With their midsummer blooms, canna are ideal for portable containers, because they can decorate the terrace or deck just as the spring parade is beginning to fade. For years, gardeners have been intimidated by their great size. But recently, new dwarf varieties have been introduced that have the canna lily's best characteristics, without the bulk.

Start canna in flats indoors at least a month before the last expected frost in the spring. Or set them out directly in containers during the spring. Be sure soil is chock-full of nutrients either by adding compost or rotted manure or by adding a complete fertilizer several times during the growing season. In the fall, dig up the rhizomes and store in dry sphagnum peat moss or vermiculite. Keep in a cool, dry storage area between 45 and 55 degrees Fahrenheit.

CHIONODOXA Hardy. Often grouped with what are known as the "minor" bulbs, chionodoxa is one of the hardiest available. Blue, star-shaped flowers with white centers occasionally break through even before the snow has left the countryside. Nothing evokes greater cheer than a tub spilling over with these low-growing bulbs. Plant in the fall in a soil mixture kept on the light, sandy side. Be sure adequate moisture is provided. Chionodoxa, which means "glory-of-the-snow," reseeds itself.

You can begin the begonia patch by planting seeds, but you'll get quicker and more reliable results by starting tubers indoors in midwinter. In February, start tubers (available at any good garden supply center) in a flat filled with moist sphagnum peat moss. Be sure the hollow, concave side is facing up and is planted so the rim of the tuber is at soil level. Keep it medium moist, not wet, because tubers are susceptible to rotting. If you can control the temperature, maintain it at 65 to 75 degrees Fahrenheit until tender plants are about three inches high. Then transplant to six-inch pots.

For the ideal potting soil, use a mixture consisting of equal parts of good garden loam, sphagnum peat moss, and compost. For added nutrients, thoroughly mix in one heaping teaspoon of steamed bone meal per gallon of soil mix.

Because the terrace pot garden may well be raised above street level, wind can be a problem for the delicately stemmed begonias. When flowers get heavy and stems long and brittle, provide support by pushing thin sticks into the pot, one for each stem. Gently tie vulnerable stalks to sticks.

As the season ends, leaves and stalks will begin to lose their vigor. Before frost, dig tubers, leaving about three or four inches of stem. Then set in sun and allow to cure. Remove stems and store in boxes filled with dry peat moss or vermiculite. Store in a cool, dry place (between 35 and 45 degrees Fahrenheit).

CROCUS Hardy. The very definition of spring hinges on the presence of the gay crocus. Tiny, cuplike blossoms often make a mockery of winter by pushing through the snow, while other plants are barely awakening. Because they're small and need little room, crocuses can be tucked into unused corners of larger tubs or planted at the base of an ornamental tree or large shrub. Or for a mass effect, devote an entire container, window box, or other planter to nothing but crocus. For the devotee, there are spring-, summer-, and fall-blossoming varieties, which, if planted wisely, will be in view throughout the growing season. Plant bulbs (strictly speaking, corms) in well-drained, porous soil in the fall. Because containers seldom get soggy, crocus will seldom be threatened by rotting.

DAFFODIL Hardy. If there is anything like a universal flower on the face of the earth, it would have to be the daffodil. Found in almost all parts of the world, the daffodil is adaptable to a wide range of soils and climates. It's so ubiquitous that it enjoys no less than three different names: daffodil, jonquil, and narcissus. But don't let labels fool you. They all refer to the same delightful flower.

People with wide-open spaces for their gardens have a field day with bulbs. Some scatter them willy-nilly for a natural effect, while others insist on carefully conceptualized borders or beds. The container grower faced with restricted space, however, has to plan carefully. But the same feeling of gay profusion can occur as easily on a patio as it does on an acre of lawn. Simply plan on six to eight containers brimming with daffodils in full flower. The pots can be linked or spaced strategically between other plants.

Because of their adaptability, daffodils are easy to grow. Simply set in a friable, well-drained soil about six inches deep. Smaller varieties don't have to be planted quite so deep. For best results, incorporate bone meal into the soil mix at planting time. A dash of compost or sphagnum peat moss will contribute to good soil structure. Water right after planting, and maintain soil moisture until the soil freezes. When choosing a container for your daffodil collection, don't skimp on size. Daffodil roots are somewhat more extensive than many other bulbs, so figure on a pot at least twelve inches deep. As with other bulbs, be sure to allow leaves to mature and fulfill their function of producing next season's nutrients. Leaves should be snipped only after they turn brown. Also, pinch off flower heads after blossoms fade to prevent seed formation.

DAHLIA Tender. The numerous shapes, sizes, and colors of dahlias can be positively mind boggling. There are ball dahlias and peony dahlias, single-flowered dahlias and anemone-flowered dahlias, pompon dahlias and even cactus dahlias. But the similarities outnumber the differences. The dahlia is a breathtaking flower consisting of tiny petals that burst into a globe-shaped blossom. For show, background, or border, dahlias are ideal.

Dahlias are generally grown from tubers that resemble sweet potatoes, with an eye at one end. Because tall stalks eventually need support, insert stakes into the container before planting the tuber. Dahlias aren't all that fussy about soil, but the growing medium ought to be well stocked with organic matter. Set the tuber in soil about five to six inches deep, with the eye next to the stake (a small shoot will emerge from the eye). But hold off planting until after all danger of frost has passed. Then, when shoots are about twelve inches tall, pinch tips to force fuller growth.

After a light frost, cut back to four to six inches and carefully lift tubers from the soil. Hose off as much soil as possible, and allow to almost dry in a shady area. Place slightly moist tubers in boxes or cartons, and cover with dry vermiculite or sphagnum peat moss. Save any dividing tasks until spring when new growth will show you where cuts ought to be made. Store in a cool, slightly moist place at 45 degrees.

ERANTHIS Hardy. Commonly called winter aconite, eranthis pushes through the cold soil in early spring and is one of the earliest of flowering bulbs. Its buttercup-shaped blossoms are barely higher than mushrooms, but its bright yellow color is hard to miss.

Fancy-leaved caladiums have no equal when it comes to attractive leaves.

Set out bulbs in late summer or fall, about three inches apart and three inches deep. They're excellent for container culture because they prefer shady locations and will do well sprinkled under and around larger evergreen shrubs. As bulbs multiply, the subtle floral display will increase. Once planted, leave them undisturbed. After flowering is complete, mulch soil lightly.

FRITILLARIA Hardy. Species of fritillaria abound, but the best for ordinary garden culture are F. imperialis and F. meleagris. Plant in rich, well-drained soil as soon as bulbs are purchased in the fall. One of the few bulbs that needs fertilizer amendments, fritillaria requires a steady diet of nutrients. Work plenty of compost into soil mix before planting, and fertilize container regularly.

GALANTHUS Hardy. Galanthus or snowdrop somehow manages to pierce even packed and frozen snow to announce the impending end of winter. Tiny, grasslike leaves become almost invisible when other plantings emerge. Because of their hardiness and small size, snowdrops do well planted underneath shrubs or at the base of vines or ornamental trees. Plant in fall and leave bulbs undisturbed.

GLADIOLUS Tender. There are over 1,000 varieties of gladiolus available, and every one offers outstanding spiked flower stalks, rich in color and form. One of the chief advantages for the gladiolus fancier is that with succession planting (corms set out every ten days to two weeks), a continuous bloom is possible. Simply schedule your plantings so a new batch is in the soil every two weeks.

In the terrace or deck garden, gladiolus can be used for background planting because stalks can grow between three and five feet high. Or, concentrate your planting in a single tub for a towering blaze of color. With a second container just planted and waiting in the wings, you can keep fresh glads nearby all summer long.

So long as the soil is well drained, gladiolus will do well (although they should also be in a sunny location). Plant corms, pointed end up, about four to six inches deep and spaced four inches apart. When stalks emerge and flower stalks begin to get heavy, provide support with stakes or string. When planted in a tub, simply insert three stakes and make a string cage by wrapping string around plants and stakes. If stakes are objectionable, try planting corms deeper than normal and hilling stalks with soil. A windy balcony or terrace, however, will mean flattened stalks unless plants are amply supported.

Allow plenty of time for leaves to mature and help form strong corms. Then, just before a frost is expected, dig corms and cut off tops. Place in shallow boxes lined with screening, and allow to cure for three weeks in a warm, dry, well-ventilated room. Then pull off old shrunken corms from the base, and carefully inspect the remaining corms. Those that

In no time, calla lilies will enliven a living area with brilliantly colored, cup-shaped blossoms and attractive leaves.

show any signs of damage or disease should be discarded to prevent spoilage of healthy corms. Then dust with a combination of fungicide and insecticide. Store in mesh bags at a temperature of 40 to 50 degrees Fahrenheit and low humidity. The better the ventilation, the less likely rot will develop.

HYACINTH

HYACINTH Hardy. Sights and sounds of spring are one thing, but the aroma of freshly opened flowers is just as invigorating. In case you have wondered where the sweet smell of spring comes from, it's the short and stubby hyacinth that perfumes the air. One of the easiest bulbs to grow successfully, hyacinth also makes an excellent companion for tulips or daffodils.

The chief ingredient of a healthy, vibrant hyacinth bed is loose, friable, and well-drained soil. When mixing soil, be sure to include ample amounts of coarse builder's sand. If you plan to move the tub from one location to another, use lightweight perlite instead of the sand. Then fill the bottom of the container with a one-inch layer of broken pot fragments, and top that with an inch or two of sphagnum peat moss. Hyacinth bulbs are planted about six inches deep and spaced four inches apart in late fall. If the container is to be left out all winter, put in a protected spot and cover with plenty of mulch. The idea is to maintain soil moisture and protect bulbs from excessive heaving, which can injure root systems.

IRIS, BULBOUS

IRIS, BULBOUS Hardy. The bulbous irises, such as Dutch, Spanish, and English, offer striking leaf forms as well as unusually formed flowers. Plant in fall in a mixture containing plenty of sand for good drainage. Bulbs should be placed four or five inches deep and spaced six inches apart. Provide mulch. After four or five years, iris will, as a rule, become crowded and will need to be divided. Gently dig up corms and rinse soil from roots and corms. Separate corms, leaving at least two buds on each section. Set in new location no deeper than about one inch. If disease is a problem, dust the corms thoroughly with a fungicide before planting.

ISMENE

ISMENE Tender. Sometimes called basket flower, spider-lily, or Peruvian daffodil, ismene has stems and leaves that resemble amaryllis but flowers that are similar to the daffodil. Quick to bloom, ismene is very sensitive to cold, so bulbs should not be set out until well after the danger of frost has passed. Plant bulbs so tips are at least three inches below the surface and spaced about 12 inches apart. In fall, dig bulbs before frost, and dry in a warm place for a week. Clean bulbs and store in a dry place between 55 and 60 degrees Fahrenheit.

LILY

LILY Hardy. No matter how extravagantly planted a garden may be, the lily with its regal splendor will almost always stand out. Tall spires with erect blossoms, the lily has earned an honored place in the world of gardening. To launch a lily bulb or two will take a little extra effort because the plant likes to have sun above but shade below, requires an acid soil, needs occasional nourishment, and doesn't like to be forced into competition with too many other growing things.

The white lily is known to practically everyone. But there are a variety of colors and forms to choose from. Most average four feet in height, while some reach seven feet. Color ranges from yellow to orange to speckled white.

More than any other bulb, the lily depends on the proper conditions for good growth. When mixing your container soil, be sure to ensure adequate drainage by placing gravel, small stones, or broken crockery in the bottom. The soil should have generous amounts of sand mixed in, as well as rotted leaf mold to contribute acidity. When purchasing bulbs, inspect them carefully to be sure you're getting healthy bulbs with undamaged roots. Then plant so the bottom of the bulb is six inches below the soil level.

As plants emerge and begin to develop, plan on several applications of a balanced chemical fertilizer (5-10-10), one when seedlings are eight inches high, the second when the first buds appear, and the third when flowering is beginning to end. A mulch over the soil will help preserve moisture and keep roots cool.

SCILLA

SCILLA Hardy. Two types of scilla are available, the Siberian squills and wood hyacinths or Spanish bluebells. Both appear in spring as a carpet of refreshing color. Siberian squills produce deep-blue, star-shaped blossoms, while wood hyacinths offer shades of pink, white, or blue and bell-shaped blossoms. Plant Siberian squills about three inches deep, spaced three inches apart. Bulbs will gradually multiply. When plants appear crowded, divide the planting. Spanish bluebells are ideally suited for interplanting with larger shrubs or trees. Plant the bulbs four inches deep in rich, well-drained soil.

TULIPS

TULIPS Hardy. Many strange stories surround the rise of the famed tulip, including the tale of the hapless trader who ate some prized rare bulbs thinking they were onions. But history aside, the tulip is perhaps the most beloved of all bulbs. The brilliant colors and graceful shapes make it one of the most popular flowers in America.

Because the tulip bulb is constantly growing and preparing for eventual bloom, it's imperative that tulip bulbs be planted in the fall immediately after they are received. Generally speaking, bulbs can be planted anytime—right up to the time the ground freezes. As with other bulbs, drainage is important, because bulbs will rot and do poorly if waterlogged. Plant at least six inches deep and water well. Be sure to inspect each day to make sure newly planted bulbs do not dry out and die as a result

Once blossoms begin to fade, pinch off any new seedpods so the bulb doesn't channel all its energy into seed formation. When taking cut flowers, be careful not to injure leaves. They're essential to bulb replenishment. With proper attention, tulip bulbs will last many years without digging, storing, and replanting.

Intrepid tulip fanciers, however, insist the best in blooms is possible only if bulbs are dug and replanted each season. There is no question that offset bulbs can crowd plants to the point where blooms are inhibited. Some growers slow offset formation by planting bulbs deeper.

Forcing Bulbs to Bloom in Winter

If the hard winds of winter have kept you house-bound and aching for a splash of color, try forcing a handful of your favorite bulbs.

First, half fill a pot that is at least twice as deep as the bulbs with a mixture of sand, soil, and sphagnum peat moss in equal amounts. If containers are large, cut down the weight by substituting perlite for sand. Place bulbs, pointed end up, on the surface of the soil and cover. Because bulbs are the plant's food source, the number of plants per pot doesn't matter, although bulbs should not be close enough to touch. After the bulbs are planted, water the container thoroughly;

label, so you know what you planted and when.

The next step is to fool the bulbs into thinking they have gone through the cold temperatures of winter. Store the pot in a cool, dark place so root growth can get under way. Temperatures should be anywhere between 35 and 50 degrees Fahrenheit. Although bulbs can stand frigid conditions, it's important the soil doesn't freeze. Also, the proper moisture level should be maintained. Once shiny green shoots appear, you can move plants into sunlight. See the chart on the next page for instructions on forcing specific bulbs.

BULB FORCING TECHNIQUES

Bulb	Potting Instructions	Forcing Instructions
Tulips	Plant six bulbs, flat side out, an inch apart. Set in a six-inch pot, with tips showing above soil.	After bulbs are planted, water pot thoroughly, and put into cold storage (a refrigerator, unheated garage, attic, or basement crawl space) for 12 weeks. Move to a cool, dark location for two weeks, then put in a sunny spot; tulips will bloom in five weeks.
Daffodils	Set six bulbs in an eight-inch pot, so they just peek out. Be sure the pot has good drainage.	After you've set daffodils in pot, water thoroughly, and put pot into cold storage for eight to twelve weeks. You can tell when the pot's ready to be taken out by checking to see if roots fill the bottom. When they do, move the bulbs to a sunny window to bloom.
Crocus	Plant ten corms in a six-inch pot. Crowd for a better display, but leave a pencil's width between.	When corms are planted, water thoroughly, and put in a refrigerator or cold closet for eight weeks. Water occasionally; check pot for root development before you take it out. Then place it in a cool room with strong light. Plants will bloom in four weeks.
Hyacinths	Use three bulbs in a six-inch pot if you're using soil; use one bulb in a vase if you're using water.	If you pot in soil, water thoroughly and put in refrigerator. (You can pot in a hyacinth vase filled with water, too.) Either way, remove from cold in seven weeks, put in partial sun one week, then move to a spot with full sun for hyacinths to bloom.
Amaryllis	Buy a treated bulb that's ready to flower. Plant in a six-inch pot, leaving half the bulb above soil.	Amaryllis doesn't need a period of cold, so set potted bulb in a sunny window or warm room with good light. Water often enough to keep the soil evenly moist. As the big stems push up, you may need to tie them to a stake for support. Let bulb rest before repotting it in the fall.
Paper-white Narcissus	Plant in a pebble-filled bowl, and add water to cover the bases of bulbs.	Store planted bowl in a cool, dark closet or basement for two weeks. Replenish the water when necessary. Then bring bowl into the sunniest location you have. The flower spikes will shoot up in a hurry, and fragrant flowers should open in three weeks.

ABCs of Trees and Shrubs

Whether a tree is a shrub or a shrub is a tree depends, as a rule, on the number of stems. Yet a shrub left to its own weedy inclinations is more than likely to stretch skyward until it looks more like a tree. And certain trees, when pruned back, become shrubs. However, one stem or a hundred, there's no doubting the usefulness of shrubs and trees as container plants.

Azalea trained in the shape of a tree serves as a dramatic container plant.

SELECTION CONSIDERATIONS

Whether grown for their evergreen foliage or spectacular blossoms, shrubs can provide instant landscaping for a terrace, patio, backyard, or deck. And they are effortless to grow. As for the tree versus shrub question, most experts agree that a tree has a single stem and is at least 12 to 15 feet tall. Anything woody with multiple, branched stems is considered a shrub.

PRICE Compared to a handful of flower seeds, though, a prize shrub or tree is somewhat more expensive. So take a moment to study your needs. Determine the amount of time you can devote to care, feeding, and eventual repotting. See what interests the family. A dwarf fruit tree or two may just inspire the whole family into sharing the container garden project. Apple, pear, plum, and peach are a few to consider.

FLOWERING VERSUS NON-FLOWERING If attractive blossoms throughout the growing season are the elusive objects of your horticultural dreams, then consider the vast selection of flowering shrubs. Some offer bold strokes of color at practically any time of year. Others, like firethorn, cotoneaster, and winterberry, produce attractive berries especially coveted by birds. Or if you have a hankering to dabble in the subtle colors and textures of leaves, plain and variegated, then opt for the evergreens. They not only provide a comforting bit of green throughout the winter months, but also form perfect background plantings for showier annual or perennial flowers. Sometimes, if you have done all your homework, you can combine the best of several worlds. Azaleas, rhododendron, and andromedas, for example, are broad-leaved evergreens that keep their leaves and explode into delicate bouquets of color and fragrance. Check the chart at the top of page 49 for an idea of the blossoming times for certain plants.

LEAF TYPES Evergreens naturally fall into two categories, depending on the growth of their leaves. Narrow-leaved types (often referred to as conifers) develop needle-like leaves, while the broad-leaved evergreens have much larger, wider leaves. Both retain their foliage throughout their dormant period, as opposed to the deciduous types, which drop their leaves every fall. As a general rule, the narrow-leaved varieties, such as pine, yew, and juniper, are a little better at surviving northern winters. Azalea, rhododendron, and holly, all broad-leaved, prefer the more temperate conditions of southern areas. But for the avid container grower, the range of choices includes practically all varieties, because planters can be moved indoors to escape the harsh conditions of winter.

SHAPE The narrow-leaved types are sometimes divided into different kinds of shapes. For most purposes, however, it simplifies things to remember that they are basically upright growers or spreading

The large, brilliantly colored blossoms of a Chinese or tropical hibiscus attractively add to the outdoor decor.

BLOSSOMING SEASONS

Consider the time of bloom. The shrewd gardener, in a kind of horticultural roulette, arranges his or her plantings according to what blossoms when. Here are some representative plants arranged by season of bloom.

SPRING	MIDSUMMER	LATE SUMMER
Azalea	Cinquefoil	Hydrangea (Peegee)
Forsythia (dwarf)	Mountain Laurel	Bush Clover
Flowering Quince	Weigela	Rose of Sharon
Andromeda	Mock Orange	Summersweet
Spirea	Hydrangea	Crape Myrtle
Tree Peony	Dogwood	

growers. Arborvitae and spruce like to grow straight up, while the creeping junipers are happy to spread out and around. When shopping at your favorite nursery, be sure to get the complete story on what you buy. To snip and clip an upright yew continually, hoping it will stay low to the ground, is a futile exercise. Better to start off with something that will naturally grow the way you want it.

Flowering shrubs also have shapes. Extra tall types, like lilacs, are just too large to thrive for long in the restricted space of containers. But medium-size, small, and low-growing shrubs, like deutzia, cinquefoil, or the ever-popular hills-of-snow hydrangea, are ideal for container culture.

TREES AND SHRUBS FOR POTTING

Selecting the right tree or shrub for a particular situation takes a bit more than wandering through the nursery and selecting the nearest one. Here's a close-up of a few of the more readily available trees and shrubs to help you find the best bush for your needs.

ANDROMEDA (*Pieris* sp.) Broad-leaved evergreen. A definite eye-catcher, sporting four-inch clusters of drooping blossoms in early spring. Rarely getting above six feet in height, andromedas will do well in full sun or partial shade but prefer a slightly acid soil. Excellent

as a specimen plant for that neglected corner of the patio or terrace. Fairly hardy but needs protection where winters are severe. Prune after flowers have faded.

AZALEA (*Rhododendron* sp.) Broad-leaved evergreen. Available in a host of varieties, ranging from all shades of white to pink. Foliage is a glossy green; flowers bloom in two- to four-inch clusters. Likes partial shade and a well-drained, acid soil. Because of its low-growing, bushy habit, azalea can be used as a spectacular hedge or as a showpiece plant. Keep shallow growing roots well mulched. Remove spent flowers shortly after bloom. Most rhododendrons are tricky when it comes to matching the proper variety to your particular hardiness zone. Consult a reliable nurseryman for the best results.

BARBERRY (*Berberis* sp.) Deciduous shrub. No more than four to six feet in height, with a dwarf form that seldom exceeds two feet. Attractive yellow flowers with red sepals appear in early spring and are followed by bright red, oval berries. Thrives in either full sun or partial shade. May be used as hedge or specimen plant.

BUSH CLOVER (*Lespedeza* sp.) Deciduous shrub. Prized because it flowers when most other shrubs have come and gone, it may hold blossoms clear into fall. Likes full sun. Cut back to the ground each

49

spring before new growth is visible. New stems will quickly appear and, at blossoming time, will reach a height of about three feet. Late-season flowering makes it ideal for containers.

CANADIAN HEMLOCK (*Tsuga canadensis*) Narrow-leaved evergreen. Best known as a hedge plant. Smaller varieties, such as Sargent's Weeping hemlock or a drawf variety, are excellent for container culture. Small, delicately formed needles give the tree a wispy appearance. Regular pruning of upright types will contribute to compact growth.

CINQUEFOIL (*Potentilla fruticosa*) Deciduous shrub. Grows to a height of four feet and is covered with yellow or white flowers from midsummer to fall. Prefers full sun. Of low-growing and dense habit, cinquefoil is hardy and fairly pest resistant. Requires little pruning. Excellent as a specimen shrub or as a low-border plant.

COTONEASTER (*Cotoneaster* sp.) Broad-leaved evergreen. Prefers slightly alkaline soil. Small pink blossoms open in early summer, followed by red berries. A low-growing, spreading plant often useful as a ground cover. In extremely cold areas, leaves will turn color and drop off. Rounded, deep green leaves offer an unusual background texture for other container plants. Gracefully formed spreading branches rarely need pruning.

DEUTZIA (*Deutzia* sp.) Deciduous shrub. Prized for its abundance of white or pink flowers so numerous they obscure the leaves and stems. Likes full sun or partial shade. Light green foliage on gently arching branches. Attractive as a specimen plant or may be planted as a low screen. Old wood should be pruned out each year. After blooming, prune new wood lightly.

DOGWOOD (*Cornus florida*) Deciduous tree. Coveted for its large white blossoms three to five inches across, dogwood makes an excellent background plant because

Primroses and nasturtiums, mingled with pansies, create a dazzling display.

it casts a light, mottled shade. Leaves turn color in the fall when most varieties form berries. Its slow growth and spreading form are especially adaptable to container growing.

FLOWERING QUINCE (*Chaenomeles japonica*) Deciduous shrub. Reaches a height of three feet or less and bears reddish-orange flowers in clusters that seem to pop out of the branches. Does best in full sun. Very little pruning necessary. In general, a low-maintenance shrub, valuable as color accent or as border plant.

FORSYTHIA (*Forsythia* sp.) Deciduous shrub. A perennial

favorite among gardeners who thirst for a touch of color as early in the spring as possible. Bright, randomly placed blossoms appear before foliage. Cascading branches that arch to the ground make the forsythia a perfect hedge plant. Dwarf varieties, such as Arnold Dwarf, are four feet high at maturity, making them good candidates for the container garden. Needs full sun or bright, mottled shade. A vigorous grower.

HYDRANGEA (*Hydrangea arborescens grandiflora*) Deciduous shrub. Often called hills-of-snow hydrangea, the three- to five-foot mature shrub explodes into huge white, globe-shaped blossoms in midsummer. Needs full sun or partial shade and a good, rich soil. Makes a showy specimen plant, or enlists its dense foliage to screen out unwanted view or wind. For medium-size blossoms, cut back bush to about two feet before new growth starts in spring. Unpruned plants will produce gigantic flowers that will bend branches almost to the ground.

JUNIPER *(Juniperus* sp.)
Evergreen tree or shrub. Available in a seemingly unending variety of types, from tall conical trees to ground-hugging creeping types, the juniper is an old standby when it comes to landscape planning. Small, scale-like needles on graceful branches give dense appearance that makes junipers ideal for planting as a windbreak. Will grow anywhere and in practically any shape.

MOCK ORANGE *(Philadelphus lemoinei)* Prized for its deliciously sweet scent that wafts through the garden in early spring. Single or double white flowers appear in early summer. Likes full sun or partial shade. Prune flower stems after blossoming because blossoms appear on old wood. Delicate flowers and deep green foliage offer effective accent colors. For hedge or border purposes, plant denser and more hardy variety, Mont Blanc.

MOUNTAIN LAUREL *(Kalmia latifolia)* Broad-leaved evergreen. Grows up to eight feet but can be kept to under four feet with judicious pruning. Delicately formed, bell-like flowers, ranging in color from white to deep pink, appear in clusters in early summer. Glossy, deep green leaves offer an interesting texture not for background planting. Does best in partial shade. For more compact growth, prune stems after flowers fade, and remove any developing seed pods.

RHODODENDRON
(Rhododendron sp.) Broad-leaved evergreen. A favorite in gardens of the Northeast because of a spectacular display of blossoms, combined with hardiness to cooler temperatures. The Carolina rhododendron reaches a height of three to four feet, which makes it suitable for container culture. Large clusters of pink-white flowers open in mid-spring. Seed pods should be removed after flowering to encourage more vigorous growth. Prefers full sun or partial shade. Must be protected from winds. Mulch heavily to protect shallow growing roots.

Above, tree-trained wisteria is the focal point for a colorful arrangement of pansies and alyssum. Right, a stately maple thrives in a container.

51

Rhododendrons do best in a slightly acid soil, so combine a good quantity of leaf mold or peat moss with the potting mix. Water rhododendrons thoroughly, checking the plants daily in hot, dry weather. Be sure to give them some shade in this weather, too.

SPIREA *(Spiraea bumalda* or *S. cantoniensis)* Deciduous shrub. Many varieties available, some up to two or three feet with blossoms white, pink, or red. Most blossom in spring or early summer. Prefers full sun or partial shade. Prune cantoniensis (Reeve's Spirea) after flowers have faded. Bumalda spirea can be pruned in early spring when plant is dormant. To prolong blossoming, trim off flowers as they fade.

YEW *(Taxus* sp.) Narrow-leaved evergreen. Second only to the juniper in popularity, the yew is a staple among landscape designers. Some are upright growers; others are conical or bushy. Still others grow only a few inches above the ground and are known as spreading yews. Dense, deep green foliage makes excellent background or hedge plantings. May be pruned or sheared at any time.

BUYING THE BUSH

When it comes to selling them, trees and shrubs are no more immune from the laws of supply and demand than anything else. As a result, the best interests of the plant are often ignored. Some trees, shipped bare-rooted, are balled and burlapped at the nursery. Although they're wrapped in a blanket of moist peat moss, careless handling can cause injury. Sometimes trees are left in the open air between changes. If not returned to the wet darkness of the soil, roots will die, leaving a corresponding batch of stems and leaves without a source of food and moisture. Most evergreens, however, because they keep their leaves the year around, have to remain in soil regardless of whether they are in transit or perched in the nursery showroom.

Roots are happiest when they are invisible, a fact that makes it difficult for the shrub shopper to determine the condition of any one plant. Ask a few questions and take a close look. With a little help from the nurseryman, you can get a good idea of what you are buying. Needless to say, it makes things easier if you have an exact idea of what you want (including the Latin name, because common names vary from one section of the country to another).

First, carefully examine the root ball to see if soil is compact and permeated with roots. If earth is loose and falls away easily, chances are the tree or shrub has recently been potted or balled and burlapped. If a tin or plastic container makes inspection difficult, ask the nurseryman to lift the plant out slightly so you can get a better look.

Next, go over the upper half of the bush and look for yellowing or spotted leaves. They may indicate past undernourishment or disease. Stems and branches should be free of breaks or deep scars. If blossoms and leaves are numerous (even if only in the budding stage) and color is good, it will probably do well after you trundle it home and plunk it into a container.

Remember, too, that size isn't everything, especially when it comes to container gardening. Often, a tree that is overgrown or has not been pruned conscientiously will have more leaves than the roots can handle. Then, after lovingly lowered into a prize container filled with premium soil, the outer branches will begin dying back. The truth is, small is beautiful when buying container shrubs and trees.

SOIL AND PLANTING

Container soil for trees and shrubs is basically the same as that used for other plants (see "Green Thumb Basics," page 74). Keep in mind, though, that tree tubs are considerably bigger and will hold much more soil, making weight a definite factor. If you plan to move your flowering shrub to several choice locations or indoors for the winter, keep soil mix on the light side. If, on the other hand, your decorating scheme calls for a thick, dense

hedge to screen an unsightly view or keep out the wind, then container weight is not a problem. The tender fruit varieties, such as peach, should be kept portable so they can be moved to a protected spot for the winter or shifted under shelter on a moment's notice when a late spring frost threatens to injure tender fruit buds.

After you buy it, place your plant in a container as soon as possible. Fill the bottom of the tub with drainage material (broken pot fragments or gravel), and cover with several inches of coarse peat moss. When working with your soil mix, be sure it is adequately moistened. If a clay pot is used, soak in water beforehand, so dry clay won't pull all the moisture out of the soil. Fill about halfway with soil, leaving a slight mound. Place the roots, if exposed, over the mound, and cover with additional soil. Hardwood shrubs and trees need hard potting, that is, soil should be almost packed into the container. Use a special potting stick made from an old hoe handle or a 1x2 to firm the soil into the container. Planting a root ball requires little more than simply lowering the plant, ball and all, into a half-filled container. Remove any loose earth, and trim off straggling or broken roots. Using a potting stick, pack the soil firmly into the space between ball and container wall. Water thoroughly. Keep the newly acquired plant out of direct sun, and protect it from the wind for a few days with a portable screen to encourage the renewal of root activity.

PRUNING AND OTHER CHORES

The principal reasons for taking out the pruning knife are:

1. Pruning keeps the tree or shrub in bounds, so it at least faintly resembles the shape you want it to have.

2. Pruning gently encourages a flowering variety to produce blossoms and not leaves.

3. Disease is kept to a minimum.

However, techniques vary somewhat, depending on whether you are snipping evergreens or flowering shrubs.

Pines are kept in bounds by simply pinching the soft, light green "candles" in half.

When trimming fine-needled evergreens, cut just above the lateral branch or bud.

For better blossoms and vigorous growth, cut out old wood and suckers when shrubs are dormant.

EVERGREENS Some evergreens can be pruned and wired into a veritable zoo of uncanny shapes, but all should be pruned to control growth and achieve proper shape. The narrow-needled types can be sheared for the "barber-shop" look, or you can snip errant or overgrown branches as they appear.

The black or mugho pine requires relatively easy pruning using just your fingers. These trees can be kept in check by pinching in half the soft, light green "candles" that sprout from the tips of the branches (see first illustration above).

To hide unsightly severed ends on other evergreens, simply make pruning cuts just inside the outer edge of the shrub where it will be concealed from view. If possible, snip just above one of the tiny leaf buds (see illustration, above, center).

If "easy care" isn't your sole goal for narrow-leaved evergreens in containers, try topiary. This means the frequent pruning of a plant to the shape of your choice—simple or complex. Yews, arborvitae, and privet are the common materials, but other heavily branched plants can be used. Plan the shape, and select an evergreen that's the full size you want. Provide a sunny spot and high-quality soil. The first year, clip all branch tips to ensure dense growth. During the second year, prune to the desired shape. If you have planned well, you should have a full globe, cube, pyramid, or more imaginative shape. Turn often to obtain even growth. Identical topiary sculptures on either side of a front

entrance are eyecatching.

Broad-leaved evergreens, such as azaleas and rhododendron, are usually pruned by removing spent blossoms to encourage branch growth or, if necessary, by the pinching off of new buds in the early spring. Old leggy rhododendrons may be rejuvenated by cutting out old limbs about six inches from the ground. New shoots will appear below the cut.

FLOWERING SHRUBS Because shrubs differ according to whether they bloom on new or old wood, pruning is either done when plants are dormant or just after flowering. Generally speaking, shrubs that offer their floral display before the end of June blossom from buds formed

during the previous year. Pruning shears should be taken in hand only after blossoms fade. Plants blossoming after June use same-season growth for their flowers and therefore may be pruned in early spring when plants are dormant (prune deciduous shrubs according to the illustration, above, right).

You can safely assume, however, that plants purchased from a nursery will have undergone plenty of pruning. More is unnecessary. Most shrubs, contrary to what you might hear, are fairly adept at keeping their own house in order. And even if your favorite bush gets a little out of hand, remember a slightly disheveled plant can add a disarming sense of informality to your outdoor sanctuary.

For a healthy formal shrub, the base must be wider than the top so light can reach the bottom to achieve dense growth that will last many years.

ABCs
of
Roses

A rose smells just as sweet, whether it sprouts from a tub, redwood planter, or an old wine cask. But fragrance is only half the story. Roses offer a gentle parade of continuous bloom; they don't shoot the works in a wild, dazzling display that fades into leafy obscurity in a day or two. The exquisite blossoms, available in an infinite variety of shapes, colors, and sizes, will, in no time, become the main attraction of your container display.

A compact floribunda rose is perfectly suited to this decorative clay pot.

WHERE, WHEN, AND HOW TO PLANT

There's no way you can hide a rose bush. Tucked away in a quiet corner or given second billing to a creeping juniper, sooner or later a blossom will emerge and thoroughly dominate the container scene. But the proper location is critical and spells the difference between healthy rose bushes and spindly under-achievers.

SUN As with many other blossoming things, roses need plenty of sunlight: at least six hours and preferably eight per day. But direct, burning, high-noon sun can adversely affect blossoms. As a result, some authorities recommend partial shade during the midday hours. With only a few minutes of careful observation, you can determine just how severe the sun is at various locations on your terrace, deck, or patio. Because containers can be shifted quickly, your roses can be given a choice location.

ROOT ROOM Roses are notorious root producers, so provide ample room for their healthy, unobstructed growth. Of course, the very nature of containers means that room to grow is limited. But by using a container of the proper size and creating a suitable soil mixture, you can meet the requirements of the most demanding roses.

WIND Decks, patios, balconies, rooftops, and terraces are prey to the wind. Unfortunately, straight streets squeezed between skyscrapers have a way of amplifying a gentle breeze into a whistling gale. Plants, however, are more accustomed to the comforting proximity of other leafy things, which not only mitigate the wind, but also reduce what otherwise would be a scorching sun. Hence, when the unprotected, containerized plants are surrounded by stone and brick, they often succumb to the unmerciful wind. The solution is simple: provide strategically located windbreaks in the form of a tall tightly woven fence, an evergreen hedge, or a built-in lath divider.

VENTILATION Insects and diseases hover continually in the wings, waiting to pounce on prize plants when the first signs of weakness appear. Dense foliage and stagnant air invite mildew and other fungi. Egg-laying insects also appreciate a quiet sanctuary, where offspring can hatch, unhampered by swirling fresh air. When arranging your plants, provide enough room for air to circulate freely.

POTTING AND REPOTTING

Whether to plant in spring or fall is a divisive argument among rose enthusiasts. However, for the container buff, the question is academic. The potted rose can be planted anytime. When and if the weather turns nasty, the rose, container and all, can simply be moved indoors.

Because rose roots need plenty of room in which to grow and develop, the container must be large enough to accommodate them. For example, a standard-size bush needs a container at least 18 inches in diameter and 18 inches deep. And no matter what the container is made of—wood, clay, or plastic—there must be good drainage,

because roses are particularly sensitive to water-logged roots. For the best drainage, drill holes at least ½ inch in diameter in the bottom of the container, and fill with an inch or two of clay-pot fragments or small stones, as in the illustration at right. An inch of peat moss over the drainage material keeps the soil from filtering downward and possibly obstructing the free flow of water. When you've decided where to put your rose, place the container on small pieces of wood or stone blocks to ensure good drainage and air circulation.

When it comes to the proper soil, there are almost as many touted soil recipes as there are rose varieties. However, roses generally thrive in most soils with plenty of nutrients and good drainage. The basic, all-purpose mix consists of one part good garden loam, one part peat moss, and one part sand. If excess weight becomes a consideration, substitute perlite for the sand. Mix the ingredients together thoroughly.

As soon as your plants are home from the nursery or garden center, set them in containers. If roots appear too extensive to fit without undue crowding, trim them back

slightly. Plant so the grafting bud is at or slightly below soil level, and fill the container to within three or four inches of the rim. Saturate with water and fill with remaining soil. If you use a clay pot, soak the pot in water beforehand to prevent dry clay from absorbing moisture from the soil. Finally, prune back canes to six to eight inches, as described on page 56. With proper care and feeding, plants should thrive in the same container for several years before repotting becomes necessary.

Tree roses flanking a natural wood entryway are complemented by handsome containers.

The sharp, angular outline of a stone sundial offers a fascinating contrast to the supple leaves and crimson red blossoms of this floribunda rose.

Because of their smaller size, miniature roses are not as demanding when it comes to container size and amount of soil. Several plants will fit into an eight-inch fern pot or other container. Taller climbers and tree types may need heavier containers or more sand in the soil mix to provide stability against stiff and gusty winds.

CARE AND FEEDING Because container-grown plants don't have the benefit of moisture-laden subsoil, adequate moisture must be provided on a regular schedule. Soil should be thoroughly drenched at least every other day. In hot, dry weather, water once a day. Arrange watering times to give foliage a chance to dry off before cooler night temperatures arrive.

Blooms and growth will be kept vigorous if a balanced fertilizer is applied on a regular basis. The first application should be worked into the top layer of soil early in the spring, when signs of new growth are visible. Work in a second dose soon after the first bloom and a final feeding about six weeks later. Any balanced fertilizer such as a 5-10-5 or a 5-10-10 (nitrogen, phosphorus, and potassium) will do. Slow-release fertilizers are especially useful, because timed release of nutrients means fewer applications. Often, a single dose is sufficient when the soil is first mixed. Or you can also combine foliar feeding with regular applications of fertilizer.

PRUNING Unchecked, roses will grow wherever a benevolent sun leads them. At the same time, spent canes will clutter the growth until your prize rose becomes a hopeless thicket. Pruning has four purposes: to remove old, spent wood; to remove surplus growth; to shape the plant; and to enhance blossoming.

The time to unsheath the pruning shears is in the spring, just after the swelling buds indicate the new season's growth is under way. Hybrid teas, floribundas, polyanthas, and some of the climbers can also be snipped just after the first bloom to remove weak lateral, inward-growing shoots. In the fall, cut plants back about one third, if they're left outside for the winter. If brought indoors, your plants will continue to grow and bloom. Miniatures, compact renditions of the classic types, are treated in the same way.

Here are some pruning tips to get your rose garden in shape:

1. Use sharp pruning shears for clean cuts. Ragged, sloppy cuts invite disease and take forever to heal, if they heal at all.

2. When pruning for shape, do it in spring or late fall. The absence of dense foliage makes the overall form easier to see.

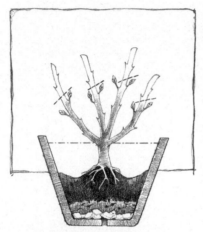

3. Make the cut through the stem about one quarter inch above an outward facing bud, as in the drawing, above. The slice should slant slightly away from the bud. This type of pruning encourages open plant growth.

4. On canes one half inch or larger, protect the plant's cut ends with a coat of ordinary pruning paint or grafting wax immediately after trimming.

5. Snip very long canes in several places, to make handling and removal easier.

6. Destroy pruned wood as soon as you complete pruning, to discourage the spread of disease to surrounding plants.

7. Because bud growth starts at the top of the plant and progresses downward (apical dominances), the more extensively you prune the bush, the later the bloom will emerge.

8. To increase the size of the primary blossoms, debud by simply pinching or rubbing off tiny side buds with your fingers.

INSECTS AND OTHER PROBLEMS If all the notorious insects and diseases were to descend suddenly on your rose patch, the plants would quickly be reduced to dust. Fortunately, with proper cultural practices, only a handful of pests will threaten them. Chief insects are Japanese beetles, whiteflies, aphids, and spider mites. Blackspot and mildew are the most common diseases attacking roses. Most insects and diseases can be kept at bay easily with the use of an all-purpose rose spray. But, if plants are given good growing conditions, their resistance to insect and disease attack will be much greater. Make sure roses get sufficient sunshine (at least six to eight hours a day) and are spaced far enough apart so air circulation is not hindered. Water as close to midday as possible, so plants will be thoroughly dry before nightfall.

THE ROSE AND ITS VARIATIONS

Over the years, horticultural tinkering with rose varieties has resulted in a host of different types. Most of these roses can be divided into distinct groupings according to their particular growth habits.

Roses grow in a fascinating array of shapes and sizes, from the pillar types (reaching almost nine feet) to the tiny miniatures (which barely break the one-foot mark). As a result, there is a rose for almost every situation—fence, ground cover, hedge, doorway, hanging basket, or raised bed. For a closer look at how your favorite roses stack up, check the chart at the bottom of page 57.

Before opting for one rose over another, become as familiar as you can with each type so you can plant the right bush in the right place.

MODERN ROSES The hybrid teas are the best known of the bush types. They offer a colorful array of double or single blossoms throughout the growing season. Somewhat cold-hardy, they will survive moderate winters if some protection is provided. Because of their upright and compact growth, the bush types are especially suited to container culture. Continual crossbreeding has produced two fairly recent forms: the low-growing floribundas, with clustered flowers and slightly greater resistance to disease, and the grandifloras, known for their blossoms and vigorous growth.

CLIMBING (PILLAR) ROSES There are differences galore when it comes to roses that ramble on and on. Some are early bloomers; others offer continuous bloom. You can also choose between varieties with large blossoms similar to the hybrid tea types or climbers that practically explode into brilliant blossom clusters. Whether large- or small-flowered, all plants are ideal as background plantings, either trained upward on a trellis or cascading over a fence or a wall. Keep in mind, however, this thicket of roses can be highly susceptible to mildew if good air circulation is not provided. Adequate spacing and good pruning will contribute to sufficient air movement.

Also included in the climbing group are varieties of roses that creep along the ground on long, supple canes. Blossoms are not quite as spectacular as other types, but the ground-hugging habit is handy for special container projects or for use as an attractive and most unusual ground cover.

MINIATURE ROSES Ideally suited to container growing, the miniature types pack all the floral glory of their larger counterparts into a delicately formed plant that rarely gets beyond 12 inches in height. Perfectly at home growing indoors or out, miniature roses are available in a wide variety of colors and are, for the most part, winter hardy.

TREE ROSES Not really a distinct type, tree roses are the result of juggling plant parts of other varieties to produce a tree-like growth. Somewhat formal in appearance, potted tree roses can become unusually ornamental when integrated with a gate, doorway, arch, or other entrance way.

OLD GARDEN ROSES By definition, any rose belonging to a class in existence before hybrid teas (1867) is considered an old garden rose. Flowers of all colors range from delicate singles to robust doubles. Many of these old-fashioned roses bloom only once a year. These traditional flowers have many virtues: charm, beauty, fragrance, hardiness, long life, and low maintenance. They are not commonly grown in containers, however.

BOOKLET AVAILABLE Each year, the American Rose Society surveys its members to establish ratings for the different varieties grown across the country.

The rating system used to evaluate each variety is based on the ten-point scale below.

10.0 perfect (never achieved)
9.0 to 9.9 outstanding
8.0 to 8.9 excellent
7.0 to 7.9 good
6.0 to 6.9 fair
below 6.0 of questionable value

The results of the annual survey are published in the "Handbook of Selecting Roses." You can obtain a copy of this booklet for 25c by writing to the American Rose Society, Box 30,000, Shreveport, Louisiana 71130. Only roses that have received a rating of 8.0 or higher are included in the listings in the booklet.

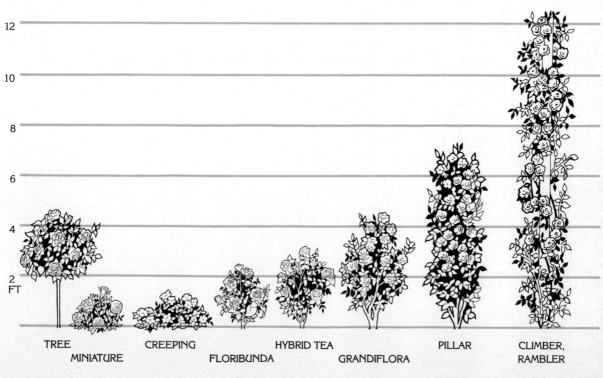

ABCs of Vines

Plants that twist and curl into pleasantly trailing vines are just as happy springing from a container as they are from the open ground. For the owner of a deck or balcony, vines are perfect for disguising pillars, poles, and other supports. Each could become a garden delight encircled by breathtaking clematis. Or a brick wall, exposed to the searing rays of the sun, can be transformed into a cool bower of gracefully climbing grape, wisteria, honeysuckle, or a spectacular rose.

Passion flower vine, although in blossom only a short time, is spectacular.

How vines manage to climb over, up, or along the nearest support is a fascinating study in adaptation. For the container grower, climbing habits are important so proper support can be provided if needed. Many vines are equipped with stringy tendrils, which grip whatever happens to be nearby. These vines are perfectly adept at finding their own support. Others twine their entire stem and hold themselves up by encircling a post or pole. Still others need help from the gardener who ties or staples them to an existing wall or other support.

As for choices, you can find a vine for almost any purpose. If a plant is to hang from wire or rest on a shelf, choose a trailing vine, such as lantana, *Vinca minor,* or English ivy. For a vertical garden, consider twining vines or woody, tendriled vines. Clematis, climbing honeysuckle, and the ever popular roses are an attractive addition to any terrace decor. The woody vines, grape and Virginia creeper, for example, although more permanent, are useful container plants. Then there are the annual vines that wind up in almost every garden, because as quick growers, they produce a breathtaking floral show in a short time. Heading the popularity list are morning glory, the tall growing nasturtiums, and some of the ornamental gourds. Some annuals, such as cucumber, squash, and melon, offer a food bonus.

CONTAINER VINES

BALSAM APPLE A rapidly growing tendril vine, balsam apple can grow as much as 15 feet in a single season. Sow seeds in large containers after the danger of frost has passed. Waxy, attractively shaped leaves complement yellow or white blossoms. They're grown sometimes just for unusual tapered fruits that burst open when ripe. Usually treated as an annual, although perennial in southern regions.

CATHEDRAL BELLS (*Cobaea scandens*) Sometimes called cup-and-saucer vine, it grows quickly to heights of 15 to 20 feet. Coveted for its large, violet blossoms on gracefully arching stems. Offers an extended period of bloom. In colder regions, it's treated as an annual.

CLEMATIS Of all the vines, clematis leads the list in popularity because of its versatility and great beauty. Useful for covering almost any surface or object with a rich curtain of foliage, dotted with large or small, exquisitely formed, star-shaped flowers. Can be a little tricky to grow because plant needs a slightly alkaline soil of good structure. Leaves and stems require plenty of sun, while roots do better in cooler, shaded soil. Often sown under a shrub where the bottom remains cool and the top can twine into sunshine. Plant seed or started seedling in container filled with soil to which sand, leaf mold, and lime have been added. Stake young plant and keep moist.

CREEPING COTONEASTER Listed by most authorities as a shrub,

Bougainvillea, with its gay profusion of flowers and climbing habit, makes a perfect container candidate.

creeping cotoneaster is often grown as a vine because of its spreading habit. Attractive tiny pink flowers cover stems. Leaves are deep green and oval shaped. Red berries make the plant an attractive winter specimen, as well as a favorite for birds. Place in sunny location, and provide well-drained soil with adequate amounts of lime.

ENGLISH IVY *(Hedera helix)* The common clinging vine that covers many a brick wall, English ivy produces rangy stems that can completely engulf a support. It can be grown up or down, cascading over a wall, or gracefully climbing a trellis. Should not be placed in direct sun but in partial or half shade. For newcomers to English ivy, purchase started plants that can be transplanted immediately into containers. If a healthy plant is accessible, cuttings can be taken and started by inserting in moist sand. Ivy likes moist soil kept on the cool side.

EUONYMUS *(Radicans vegetus)* One of the hardiest of evergreen vines and simple to grow because it will survive in practically any soil. Leaves are oval shaped and sometimes variegated. Grown mostly for foliage. Other varieties are compact in growth and useful as trailing ground covers.

GOURDS, ornamental. Unfailing curiosities because of their strange fruit, the ornamental gourds make attractive climbing vines as well. Plant from seed in rich, well-prepared soil after the danger of frost has passed, and keep container moist. Rapidly growing vines will need support either in the form of stakes or an existing fence. Lush, thick-leaved vines can be an instant screen for an unsightly view.

GRAPE The domestic varieties are the hardiest and the most practical for home container growing. For profuse vines and lush foliage, stems may be allowed to spread at will. But if fruit is desired, canes will have to be trained and pruned to ensure greatest production. Make sure container soil is well drained (add sand or perlite, if necessary)

and complemented with rotted cow manure or compost. As vines begin to expand, provide some support for tendrils to wind around.

HONEYSUCKLE, climbing *(Lonicera* sp.) Available in many varieties, the vining honeysuckles are prolific growers and adaptable to a wide range of soils and conditions. Flowers are tubular or bell-shaped. Berries are white or red, fleshy, and appealing to birds. For best results, use a rich, well-structured soil and keep moist. Plant from seed or seedling vines.

HYDRANGEA, climbing *(Hydrangea petiolaris)* Offers a multitude of showy flowers. Large, oval-shaped leaves with globular blossoms, usually white and borne in clusters. Clings well to masonry or brick.

LANTANA, trailing *(Lantana sellowiana)* Although vine-like in growth, does not grow to great heights and therefore is more suitable where medium-sized plants are needed or as a trailing specimen. Have proven themselves ideal as potted plants.

NASTURTIUMS Commonly grown as an annual, the taller varieties will grow as high as eight to ten feet. The soft-stemmed vines curl and twine themselves around the nearest support. Flowers are bright yellow-orange or sometimes scarlet or red. Avoid temptation to use rich soil because overfed nasturtiums will produce all leaves and few flowers.

ROSES, climbing For spectacular beauty throughout the growing season, the climbing roses should be included in every container garden (see "Roses," page 57).

WISTERIA *(Wisteria floribunda or W. sinensis)* Although requiring more care and patience, wisteria produces such exquisite vines and flowers that any extra effort is worthwhile. Place young plant in a container filled with rich, humusy soil. Water generously throughout first season of growth. Tie emerging vine to a support.

59

ABCs of Fruit

For the ultimate in backyard food growing, nothing matches the challenge of nurturing a tiny orchard of choice fruit trees. Even though there are a few growing difficulties, the rewards defy description. A sun-ripened peach fresh off the stem has absolutely no equal in flavor. An apple just picked from the tree is similar only in name to the super-market variety. Plums, cherries, grapes, pears, apricots, and blueberries are other good container candidates.

Dwarf peach trees offer attractive foliage and a bonus of delicious fruit.

Fruit growing is not without problems, however. Bugs hover in the air, waiting to get first crack at the ripening fruit. Birds, ever on the lookout for ripe berries, swoop down to pluck the tree clean. Fingers of frost often linger after all thoughts of winter have vanished to freeze tender buds and render them impotent.

However, as old-timers will tell you, conditions are everything. If you're tempted to get a miniature orchard under way on your terrace, be sure to study as thoroughly as you can the requirements of each fruit. It's literally fruitless to force an apple to grow like a grape or expect a peach to survive where only a blueberry bush will grow.

SUN There is little you can do to shortcut the need for sun. All fruits need sunshine. But container growers are often more fortunate than the backyard grower, because a tree can be put on wheels and kept in constant sunshine. At the same time, if a late frost threatens, tree—container and all—can be rushed into the garage or breezeway where it can ride out the weather. Or, because trees are dwarf, a sheet, a piece of plastic, or an old blanket can be thrown over the branches to protect it from the wicked cold.

SOIL Most fruits do best in soil that is slightly acid. Blueberries are unique in that they require even greater acid conditions. Most soils exposed to average rainfall are naturally acid, but if you suspect your container soil is neutral or on the alkaline side, it's easy to sour things a little by mixing in powdered sulfur, following the manufac-turer's directions.

DRAINAGE Whatever fruit you decide to grow, good drainage is essential. Again, the container buff has a head start because soggy soil is seldom a problem. But that doesn't mean the requirement can be ignored. Check the container for an adequate number of holes, and drill extras if necessary. Also plenty of broken crockery or small stones should cover the bottom before the soil mix is put in.

POLLINATION Oddly enough, many fruit trees are unable to pollinate themselves, which means another variety of the same fruit must be planted nearby for the blossoms to set fruit. If bees are scarce, the homeowners may have to take matters into their own hands and pollinate the fruit tree themselves. The important thing is to query your nurseryman and find out which trees are self-pollinating and which are not.

INSECTS The number of bugs that whiz and dart over the countryside is staggering. And many are as fond of fruit trees as we are. But modern chemistry offers some effective and safe remedies, if they're used carefully and intelligently. Once your trees are established, check the nearest garden supply center for an all-purpose spray, and apply exactly as the manufacturer suggests.

SIZE When browsing through a nursery for a fruit tree, be sure to purchase a tree with a dwarf root stock that will grow no higher than six to eight feet. The height will vary with the variety you grow, but it's important that your tree isn't too big for container growing.

PLANTING There is no better reminder of frontier America than an apple tree covered with a dome of aromatic blossoms. With advances in breeding and grafting, it's possible to enjoy the glory of fresh-grown fruit without having to establish a full-fledged orchard. Dwarf root stock makes it possible to grow old favorites, but on a miniature scale. For best results, have your container filled with soil and ready to go before you bring your tree home from the nursery. Avoid damage to roots from the wind and the drying effects of direct sun by planting right away. If some delay is necessary, store in a cool cellar after soaking roots thoroughly. Make sure soil is open and porous so water can flow through freely and, at the same time, retain enough to supply roots. If necessary, mix ample amounts of sphagnum peat moss with good garden loam to improve soil structure. Set in tree, making sure the grafting bud is at least one or two inches above soil line. Carefully pack soil in and around roots, so no air pockets remain. Then water. After the water has saturated the container and the soil has settled, inspect the tree trunk to make certain the bud graft (look for a bulge where tree and root stock have been joined) is above soil level.

If wind regularly sweeps your terrace or patio, the young tree will get off to a better start if you provide some means of support. Either push a stake directly into the container, or place the tree next to a pillar or other support. Later on, when the tree begins to bear fruit, the stake will come in handy for supporting fruit-laden branches. If wire is used, prevent chafing of the bark by threading the wire through a small loop of old garden hose.

As a rule, new trees are pruned slightly to match the leaves' demand for food with the capabilities of the root system. All that's needed is a gentle thinning out of branches and perhaps cutting back of extra vigorous shoots. After planting, peach and cherry trees are often more severely pruned than are apple trees.

CARE AND FEEDING Once the tree is planted and on its own, not much is required in the way of feeding, provided the soil is properly prepared prior to planting. However, fruit trees respond well to applications of organic soil conditioners, well-rotted compost or manure, for example. Mulching also is a good practice to develop, because it helps increase nutrient content of the soil, conserves moisture, and maintains even soil temperatures. Spread a three- to six-inch layer of salt hay, grass clippings, or peat moss around base of tree. If a commercially prepared fertilizer is used, apply sparingly. Too much may result in excessive foliage growth. The best time to feed fruit trees, whether you use manure, compost, or a commercial preparation, is in early spring.

Insects and disease can play havoc with the best tended of fruit trees if not kept in check. Container gardeners, however, find insect and disease scourges less of a problem because diversified planting and good ventilation are built into the terrace or patio garden. But certain precautions still must be taken to ensure quality fruit. Spraying must be done regularly. You can use a dust or soluble form of insecticide. Spraying, however, is usually recommended because the tree is more thoroughly covered and there is less danger of the material drifting to affect other plants or threaten children and pets. Several all-purpose preparations are available. Follow manufacturer's directions to the letter.

One of the most menacing enemies of fruit trees is freezing temperature. If cold penetrates tiny buds as they begin to swell in the spring, the yield could be drastically reduced. When spring arrives, keep an eye on the thermometer, and protect the tree by moving it inside or by covering it with plastic. Peaches and apricots are especially susceptible to lower temperatures.

PRUNING If you're a beginning fruit grower about to do some pruning, keep in mind why pruning is important, so trees are helped instead of hindered. Basically, pruning is undertaken to enhance the fruit-bearing qualities. This means taking out old or misshapen branches, as well as those shoots that crowd other branches. Weak wood, which is easy to identify because it is thin and tends to droop downward, will only produce inferior fruit—if it produces at all.

Use sharp tools when trimming your tree, and reserve all pruning chores for a period when the tree is dormant, either in late winter or very early spring. Make cuts just above outward facing buds and at a slight angle. If a sucker or lateral branch is removed, make the cut as close as possible to the main stem, so no stub remains. Unless a resulting wound is two inches or more in diameter, no additional treatment is necessary, because trees will heal nicely by themselves.

Once tiny fruits begin to form, thin them a bit, because fruit trees have a tendency to set more fruits than the tree can handle. If the tree is left to its own devices, fruits will be small and of poor quality. Branches with too much fruit might actually break off.

Growing Food in Containers

Just because your backdoor doesn't open onto a sun-filled vista with thousands of square feet of soil doesn't mean homegrown vegetables aren't possible. Fortunately for the gardener who has little space to work with, soil is something that can be made at home. All you have to do is gather the ingredients, repair to the cool security of your cellar or closet, and simply mix up a batch yourself. A time-tested formula calls for equal parts of sphagnum peat moss, soil, and sand. If pots are to be shifted, substitute perlite for the sand.

Or, if alchemy isn't one of your strong points, buy a bag of potting soil at a garden supply center. Then fill a container or two, and sow your favorite vegetables. Remember, though, most fruiting crops, such as cucumber, melon, and tomatoes, need lots of sun. Leaf crops grown for their leaves, such as lettuce, Swiss chard, mustard, collards, corn salad, and even beet greens, can tolerate a smattering of shade.

Anything that will hold soil can be used as a container. Old kitchen pots, cake pans, plastic hampers, wood baskets, clay pots, or even an old sink will do. If you have scrap lumber, make your own containers. The mobile mini garden pictured on the opposite page is easy to build and light enough to put on wheels. Overflowing with salad crops, such as lettuce, chives, cherry tomatoes, radishes, and bunching onions, the unit can be kept in full sun all day. The six-foot troughs, constructed of treated wood, are filled with a lightweight soil mix.

Whatever you grow in your containers, keep two critical requirements in mind. One of the primary functions of soil is to give roots something to hold onto, so plants can stay upright. And the windier your terrace, deck, or balcony is, the heavier the soil mix should be. For example, if you envision a grove of eggplants on top a 30-story building, plan on deep containers weighted with an ample amount of the proper soil mixture to give plenty of room for root growth.

Container soil dries out quicker because, unlike topsoil, it can't soak up moisture from the water table through capillary action. Therefore, water at least every other day (every day during dry, hot spells), and make sure the soil you use is able to retain a large amount of water. Sphagnum peat moss, perlite, vermiculite, and rotted compost can hold considerable amounts of water. Sand, on the other hand, holds practically no water.

Here's a sampling of crops that are especially adaptable to container growing.

BEETS Beets offer two rewards. Not only are the roots edible, but the greens are a gourmet's delight, as well. Plant seeds about ½ inch deep as soon as you can manipulate the container soil. To aid germination, cover seeds with sifted sphagnum peat moss or vermiculite. When seedlings are four inches high, thin to three inches apart.

CARROTS Juicy, perfectly-formed carrots are a cinch for the container gardener because the soil is custom mixed and is therefore free of obstructions that normally deform roots. Plant seeds about ½ inch deep, either in small rows or in clumps, then thin to two inches apart when plants are three inches high. Buy shallow-rooted varieties.

CUCUMBERS Because of their long, trailing vines, cucumbers can be attractive patio or terrace plants as well as a source of food. If space

Where there is sun, there can be a gathering of vegetables seasoned with herbs.

is at a minimum, encourage vines to grow on supports. Most cucumber growers start seed indoors well before the snow melts. Established plants are then transplanted to the container after the danger of frost has passed.

EGGPLANT Once the velvety leaves and lavender blossoms of eggplant have appeared, you'll find it compares easily with any of your prize ornamental flowers. For best results, purchase healthy seedlings at a garden supply center, and transplant into the container as soon as the threat of frost has passed.

LETTUCE A cool-season crop that can tolerate partial shade, lettuce offers intriguing leaf color and texture, in addition to delicious salad greens. The loose-leaf types are best because outer leaves can be picked as they develop, while center leaves are left to mature for later pickings. Sow as soon as soil will permit, or start seed indoors for an extra-early crop. For a continuous supply, plant a new batch every ten to 14 days. Other leaf crops suitable for containers are Swiss chard, spinach, mustard, and dandelion.

ONIONS To make your garden of food complete, plan on a handful of easy-to-grow onions. Requiring little space, they can be grown from sets or directly from seed. Make sure soil is kept moist.

POTATOES A bushel basket spilling over with potato vines is an eye-catcher that offers bushels of fun for the entire family. In the fall, when vines begin to die back, fresh spuds can be dug and prepared.

TOMATOES Garden inch for garden inch, few vegetables provide so much as the popular tomato. Easy to grow, either from seed or from seedlings, tomatoes also offer a wide range of varieties, from dime-size cherry tomatoes to huge, vitamin-rich beefsteak types. The cherry tomatoes are especially handy for hanging baskets. Simply fill the container with soil mix fortified with plenty of compost, well-rotted manure, or fertilizer, and plant the seeds.

This portable mini garden consists of treated wood fastened securely to a 2x6 frame. Because the rack is on wheels, emerging plants can be turned so the sun is always available. Troughs are filled with nutrient-rich soil mix of equal parts sphagnum peat moss, garden loam, and perlite.

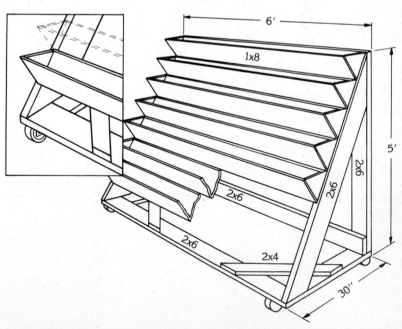

V-shaped troughs, left, made from 1x8s are securely attached to a 2x6 frame. Heavy-duty casters add mobility. Stepped 1x8 wooden troughs, right, are nailed securely to frame. Use rust-resistant nails or screws for best results.

Growing Vegetables Hydroponically

For prehistoric humans, the popping of green plants out of a brown and seemingly barren land was nothing less than magic. Their developing minds recognized seemingly miraculous connections between the sun and vegetation. To explain them, they relied upon a complex order of gods and goddesses. Today, things are different. Of course, not everything has been explained, but scientists have been able to isolate many of the elements that contribute to plant growth. And ever since, experimenters have tinkered with methods of growing things without the need for soil.

The result has been nutriculture, the art of growing plants in an artificial medium.

The idea is to bypass the complicated chemical exchanges taking place in ordinary soil and simply make the crucial nutrients directly available to plants. One way to do this is to set plants in an artificial aggregate soil, such as perlite, vermiculite, or sand, and then add a specially prepared nutrient solution. Or the "non-soil" can be eliminated altogether and the plants grown hydroponically by suspending roots in the nutrient solution itself.

For the container gardener, nutriculture can offer bonanza yields with maximum use of available space. With proper support, plenty of light, and conscientious care, a small jug can support a six-foot tomato vine. Most garden supply centers stock prepared nutrient mixes containing the critical major, minor, and trace elements required for healthy plant growth. The more adventurous may obtain separate ingredients and custom mix their own solution.

For healthy growth, vegetable plants are no different than any other plant. Like other plants, they too need nitrogen for lush leaf growth; phosphorus for blossoming, fruiting, and root growth; and potassium for good stem development and disease resistance. But besides the fact that we eat food crops, there is another important difference—size. Vegetables need room. Vine crops especially like to creep and roam at will, while tomatoes and beans like plenty of space. Here's where hydroponics fits in. Because nutrients are directly available, only a fraction of the normal space is needed. Vines, of course, will have to be gently encouraged to grow on supports, but you'll find the yield per cubic foot of space is many times greater. If you're willing to take hammer in hand, the possibilities are limited only by your imagination. One approach is to squeeze a mini-farm into your container landscape by constructing a double tiered 1½ x 3-foot box out of kiln-dried redwood. Line each tier

A pump and timer automatically keep this mini-farm supplied with nutrients.

with 20 mil vinyl, so the bottom can hold nutrient solution, while the top tier is filled with lightweight artificial soil. For early- and late-season vegetables, you can add a greenhouse canopy to trap sun and keep out cold.

ARTIFICIAL SOIL

For the novice, using a soilless material is an ideal introduction to nutriculture because an aggregate material such as washed sand, gravel, vermiculite, or perlite allows for proper air penetration and plant support. At the same time, the nutrient solution can wash freely around the suspended roots without eliminating all available air.

Any container will do, so long as there is provision for proper drainage. Punch or drill holes if necessary in the bottom, and cover with cheesecloth or other netting so growing material will not be flushed out. Fill pot to within a half inch of rim with artificial soil and tamp gently. Start seeds in a separate flat, and then shift to nutriculture container when they're large enough to transplant without injury.

There are several ways nutrient solution can be applied:

1. "Slop" or top watering. Once the solution has been mixed, simply apply to top of container—as you would ordinary water—once or twice a day, depending on the strength of the solution. A container should be placed beneath the drainage hole to catch excess liquid. Usually, a batch of nutrient solution can be used several days before a new preparation is needed. Old solution may be used to water the lawn or outdoor garden.

A variation of the top watering technique makes plant care somewhat automatic, allowing you to leave plants unattended for several days at a time. Place a container of nutrient solution above the level of the topsoil in the plant pot, and connect tubing so liquid can be either gravity-fed or siphoned. A clamp attached to the tubing will regulate the flow so that just the right amount is provided.

2. Wick System. Another method provides bottom feeding by using a glass wool wick dipped in a second

container filled with the nutrient solution. The end inserted in the artificial soil is spread out so nutrients are distributed evenly throughout the container. The wick is then passed through the drainage hole into a second container filled with liquid. Or several wicks can be used to supply liquid to a plant tray set within a second tray.

3. Bucket lift method. A quick-and-easy way to provide daily

BUCKET AND TRAY

saturation of nutrient solution is to connect the bottom of a pail to the bottom of a plant box or tray with tubing and then fill pail with nutrient solution. Once a day, lift pail above soil level until the surface soil becomes well moistened. Then lower pail so excess can drain back into reservoir.

4. Or you can automate your hydroponic project by connecting a

PUMP AND TIMER

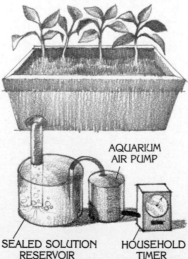

SEALED SOLUTION RESERVOIR   HOUSEHOLD TIMER

AQUARIUM AIR PUMP

timer-activated pump to the nutrient tank. When the pump goes on, solution is forced into the plant box. When it goes off, unused liquid drains back into the nutrient tank.

Whatever method you use, the nutrient solution should be shielded from light, to retard growth of algae and other organisms.

WATER CULTURE (HYDROPONICS)

The hydroponic grower suspends the plant roots directly in the nutrient solution. The problem is providing sufficient air. Sometimes an inch or two of air space is left between water level and the crown of the plant so these roots can take up the necessary oxygen to satisfy the plant's needs. Or, a fish tank aerator is connected to the nutrient container. Because roots are submerged in the nutrient solution, care must be taken to provide the correct mixture, as well as maintain the proper pH level.

RECYCLING PUMP

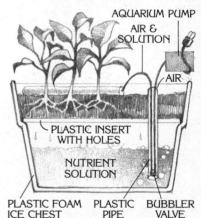

AQUARIUM PUMP
AIR & SOLUTION

AIR

PLASTIC INSERT WITH HOLES

NUTRIENT SOLUTION

PLASTIC FOAM ICE CHEST   PLASTIC PIPE   BUBBLER VALVE

Once seeds have sprouted and seedlings have developed true leaves, they may be held in place with cotton wadding or supported in a litter material, such as excelsior or wood shavings. For litter growth, construct a wire mesh basket and suspend over the solution. For seedlings, allow a half inch to one inch of air space between water level and plant crown and anywhere from two to three inches for mature plants. As in artificial soil culture, paint or wrap nutrient solution containers to keep out the light.

65

Rooftop Vegetables

With a handful of good-size containers, a little bit of know-how, and a packet or two of seeds, you can transform a hot roof into a miniature farm. Use tubs made from wooden nail kegs for the tomato patch, small trough-like containers for herbs, and ceramic pots for select vegetables, like lettuce and other greens. Or, you can fashion raised beds for roving vine crops, squash, melons, and cucumbers, for instance. If the roof is small, plan on training vines or other creepers to grow up wire, string, or wood supports. Or, you can let ranging vines droop over a railing or wall.

The first step is to check with the owner of your building to make certain the structure will support the extra weight. Containers and soil, especially wet soil, can add up to considerable weight. But you can cut down on poundage by using plastic containers and a specially mixed lightweight soil, such as equal parts of garden loam, sphagnum peat moss, and perlite.

Chances are the rooftop will be bathed in sun almost all day, which means your vegetables will get the six to eight hours they need. If part of your elevated mini farm is in shade, don't despair. There are plenty of shade-tolerant food crops that will thrive with as little as four hours of sun each day. As a general rule, plants that produce above-ground fruits need all the sun they can get, while leaf and root crops can get by on much less sun.

Vegetables, though, need good rich soil, so plan on a bag or two of dried cow manure or compost to mix with your potting soil. Here are just some of the vegetables you can raise in your rooftop garden.

BEANS Beans offer delectable flavor and a wide variety of types and sizes. There are beans for frying, boiling, sauteing, drying, baking, and even stringing.

To enjoy a continuous harvest, plan on succession planting every ten to 14 days. For the container gardener, the pole varieties are more advantageous than bush types because they can be trained on supports. Plant seeds about three inches apart after all danger of frost has passed. Place the container next to a wall or fence so vines will have support. After seeds have sprouted and are established, pinch out the weaker plants, so remaining plants stand about six inches apart. Beans are adaptable to a wide variety of soil conditions. However, container soil will dry out rapidly, so be sure water is provided as soon as the surface feels dry to the touch. Apply supplementary feeding throughout the growing season.

CUCUMBER If there are tomatoes in the garden, then cucumbers are a must. For flavor and ease of growing, cucumber has earned a place as one of the most popular homegrown vegetables. Its trailing growth makes it ideal for a rooftop garden. A tender vine, cucumber needs a warm soil and freedom from frost. Plant seeds eight inches apart, and later thin to 12 inches apart. Provide supports in the form of stakes or trellis. Pick fruits as soon as they are the desired size.

EGGPLANT With its velvety leaves and attractive lavender blossoms, eggplant looks as good as it tastes. A long-season, tender vegetable, eggplant will do well where there are warm days and nights. Either start seed indoors, or purchase seedling plants from a garden supply center and then transplant to the container after all the danger of frost has passed. Gradually introduce it to outdoor conditions by setting the plant outside during the day and inside during the night. Keep soil well fertilized and watch for injurious bugs. Fruits are ready for picking at almost any stage, but be sure skins are still glossy.

LETTUCE Easy to grow and undemanding, lettuce is perfect for container culture. Lettuce is a hardy crop the seeds of which can be dropped into the soil as soon as you can get a trowel into it. Plant seeds indoors for an early crop, or plant directly into the container. Space about one inch apart. Once seedlings emerge, thin so plants have ample growing room. For lush green leaves, fertilize occasionally with fertilizer high in nitrogen. Loose-leaf types provide continuous picking—select outer leaves, and the center will produce new ones.

MUSKMELON Muskmelon can present a few challenges because it is a long-season crop and fairly sensitive to radical changes in temperature. Growers with short seasons usually start seed indoors or purchase seedlings from a nursery. Plant seeds only after the danger of frost has passed and the soil has had a chance to warm thoroughly. Thin to two or three healthy plants per pot. Provide support when vines begin to form. Remember, when fruits reach the picking stage, they can become heavy enough to snap vines. Make slings from nylons or cheesecloth and nail to supports.

PEAS Without question, peas need the cooler temperatures of early spring and fall to develop properly. Their attractive foliage and bright white flowers make them more than just an ordinary vegetable crop. Plant seeds about two to three inches apart as soon as the container soil can be worked. Taller varieties will need some form of support. Pick pods before outer skins become tough and leathery.

PEPPER Because of the time required for pepper to mature and set fruit, purchase healthy seedlings from a garden supply center, or start your own plants by sowing seeds in flats indoors. Tender plants, peppers should not be transplanted to the outdoor container until all danger of frost has passed. Adaptable to a variety of soils, peppers require little fertilizer. Fruits are ready at any stage of development.

RADISH For economy of space and quick growth, the lowly radish takes all honors. They seem custom made for the container gardener, because you can have fresh radishes long before anything else is even poking up a leaf. Simply scatter seed in soil as soon as it can be worked. Thin to two inches apart. Because quick growth is the key to successful radish growing, it pays to maintain soil moisture and provide an occasional dose of fertilizer. Pick when roots are juicy and tender.

SPINACH A hardy vegetable, it can be planted as soon as the soil is ready. Plant seed ¼ inch deep and then moisten soil thoroughly. Thin seedlings when necessary. Mature plants should be four or five inches apart. As with leaf crops, spinach responds well to applications of a fertilizer high in nitrogen. Outer leaves may be picked as needed, or you can harvest the entire plant.

TOMATOES The tomato can be found in more gardens throughout the country than any other vegetable. In terms of yield, few plants will give you more for your time and money. A long-season crop requiring warm days and nights, tomatoes are usually started inside, hardened off, and then transplanted outdoors when all danger of frost has passed. Or, plants may be purchased. When preparing soil for tomatoes, work in generous amounts of dried manure, compost, or other organic material. The natural bush growth makes it ideal for tub or hanging baskets.

As plants become established, you'll notice sucker stems emerging from the point where the leaf branch joins the main stem. For more rigorous fruit development, pinch off suckers. Feed occasionally with a commercial fertilizer. When fruit begins to turn pink, watch carefully so tomatoes can be enjoyed at peak ripeness. Fruit should practically fall into your hands when you pick it. As season nears its end, pinch back new growth so the existing fruit ripens. If the container is portable, you might want to wheel your tomato patch indoors where the plant should continue to produce.

SQUASH The winter squashes are notorious for consuming space, but with a little imagination, you can coax vines to grow between other containers or climb a nearby fence or trellis. With breeders constantly searching for better varieties, new bush types are available. Compact growth plus high yield make them ideally suited for gardening in small spaces. All the squashes are tender and should be planted only after the threat of frost has passed. Because plants are very large, plenty of soil nutrients are needed. Work dried cow manure or compost into the soil mixture.

Formerly a cement wasteland, this rooftop is now a money-saving paradise of fresh vegetables, all grown in containers.

How to Grow Vegetables Indoors

More often than not, the patio, deck, or balcony is where home gardeners put their best plant forward. Exotic blossoms, blazing with color, reign in isolated splendor, inviting guests and gardener alike to set aside the day's worries. By the time these spectacular ornamentals have claimed the outdoor living area, there isn't a square inch left for a vegetable or herb. But that doesn't mean growing food has to be postponed. With clever planning and a sun-splashed window, you can raise a rewarding assortment of vegetables indoors. And better, by sharing the indoors with plants, you can enjoy fresh produce all year, regardless of the season.

Vegetables, considering the space needed to grow them, are clumsy leviathans compared to the petite browallia or wax begonia. But recently, breeders have made giant leaps in developing miniature varieties that produce the same vegetables but on smaller plants. Patio Pick and Bush Whopper, for example, are two compact versions of cucumber. Both develop bush plants with little reduction in yield. Even the sprawling winter squashes have been tamed. Golden Nugget and Butterbush are only one quarter the size of their gargantuan parents.

SUN There is one thing, however, that breeders have not been able to change: the amount of sun required. No matter what you grow or where, you'll have to arrange things so your indoor food crops get plenty of sun—at least six hours per day. Therefore, a sunny window, facing south, is a must. If shade seems to have claimed the house, look for ways to increase light by removing drapes, painting interior walls a reflective color, or trimming outside foundation plants that hinder sunlight. If you have some spare lumber handy, try building a special reflective screen that can be moved as the sun moves across the sky. If sunlight is scarce, it doesn't mean all your plans for homegrown food have to be scratched. You can easily supplement existing light by using fluorescent fixtures. As a general rule, plan on about 20 watts of light per square foot of growing area. You can use special grow bulbs or rely on a combination of cool white and warm white. By installing a timer, your artificial sun will go on and off precisely when you want it to, providing just the right amount of light plants need for healthy growth.

TEMPERATURE A common problem affecting indoor plants is drying out. Many homes, kept at constantly high temperatures, soon become insufferable hotboxes for plants. It's a matter of simple physics. Outside air seeps inside and expands as it is heated. Because the moisture content has not changed, the air becomes much drier. When too dry, it will actually pull moisture from the plants, causing them to wilt and eventually

Good food can be grown easily indoors, providing there is plenty of sun.

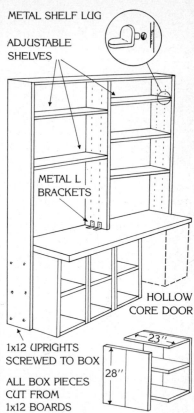

METAL SHELF LUG

ADJUSTABLE
SHELVES

METAL L
BRACKETS

HOLLOW
CORE DOOR

1x12 UPRIGHTS
SCREWED TO BOX

ALL BOX PIECES
CUT FROM
1x12 BOARDS

23"

28"

Growing shelves in a sun-splashed window are easy to build and ideal for a host of sun-loving vegetables and herbs, plus a flower or two.

die. So, keep your indoor vegetable patch away from radiators and other sources of heat. One good way to maintain humidity is to mist plants occasionally with a hand-held mister made especially for the purpose. A tray or bowl of water placed in the vicinity of your plants is also helpful. If conditions are severe, you might consider installing a portable humidifier.

As for temperature, plants are tougher than most people think. Remember, though, that fruiting vegetables, such as tomatoes and cucumbers, need warmth for blossoms to set and fruiting to occur. Ideally, the temperature should hover between 60 and 70 degrees Fahrenheit. Keep in mind, too, that the temperature near a window can drop close to the freezing point on a bitterly cold night. Insulate by placing a sheet of plastic over the window. Or move plants away when the weather threatens to turn extremely cold. To keep track of conditions, hang a thermometer near the plants.

SOIL When you consider just how much a vegetable plant grows in producing roots, stems, leaves, and finally edible fruit, it's clear that abundant nutrients are needed. Coupled with growth, is the fact that plants, ordinarily grown in acres of soil, are suddenly plunked into a thimbleful of soil practically suspended in mid air. As a result, soil temperatures are warmer, and moisture loss through evaporation is much higher. Check containers every day, and water generously if the soil surface feels dry.

Plants will wither and droop if roots are kept wet and soggy, so drainage is important. Whatever container you use, provide holes for drainage. As a rule of thumb, there should be one ¾-inch hole for every square foot of bottom area.

The ideal soil for vegetables is rich in humus and, at the same time, is loose enough to allow for proper drainage. If this is your first attempt indoors, it might pay to buy commercially prepared potting soil from a garden supply center. In small amounts, these scientifically formulated artificial soils are economical, germ-free, and easy to use. It's also possible to mix your own soil by combining equal amounts of sphagnum peat moss, garden loam, and sand. To keep nutrient levels high, mix in well-rotted compost, dried cow manure, or a slow-release chemical fertilizer. Or you can eliminate soil altogether by growing plants hydroponically (see pages 64 and 65). Once soil is in the containers, sow seed directly into the pot or into flats for later transplanting.

69

ABCs of Herbs

Gardeners haven't earned their horticultural wings until they have learned to appreciate the subtle qualities of herbs. Tiny blossoms on thin, delicately formed stems sometimes make an herb barely distinguishable from a weed. Yet pinch a leaf and partake of the delicious scented oils, and you'll be an herb lover forever. Containers offer almost perfect conditions for herbs, because drainage is excellent and the portable tubs make plenty of sunshine possible. Your herbs can follow the sun.

Herbs are not only attractive, but also offer a potpourri of delicious flavors.

All is not lost, however, if sun is scarce. Some herbs will tolerate partial shade. Try woodruff, with its attractive star-shaped blossoms and light green leaf whorls. Lovage, a tasty ingredient in salads and soups, will thrive in less than full sunshine, as will parsley, sweet cecily, ginger, oregano, and chervil. Often considered the ragamuffins of the herbs because of their rank, undisciplined growth, the various mints are ideal for the confined quarters offered by containers. Keep a clump of lemon balm or spearmint close to the kitchen door for delectable additions to summer drinks.

Whether an herb pops up each season on its own accord or has to be planted from seed each year depends on whether it is a perennial or annual. Perennial herbs come up each year, while annuals need to be sown each spring. Chives, tarragon, woodruff, mint, cicely, catnip, marjoram, rosemary, sage, dandelion, and thyme are some of the popular perennials. But just because a perennial persistently sprouts each year doesn't mean it can be neglected. Harsh winters, together with excessive heaving of the soil, can destroy an herb garden. Move herb pots to a protected area or cover with a deep mulch.

Annual herbs, on the other hand, need to be started from scratch each season. Dill, chervil, borage, coriander, fennel, basil, and parsley are some of the popular annuals. Technically speaking, parsley and dill are biennials: plants become established the first season and set seeds the second season. Most, however, are treated as annuals.

When harvesting herbs, try to time your picking so leaves or flower heads are gathered when flavor is at its peak. Generally, leaves should be harvested just before flower buds begin to open, especially if leaves are slated for drying and storage. Also, try to restrict picking to the morning hours before the hot midday sun dries surface oils. Place leaves on a rack constructed of a wire screen nailed or stapled to a wood frame, or simply spread on a cheesecloth hammock. When leaves are thoroughly dried, place in airtight bottles or plastic containers. For the best flavor, store containers in a cool place out of direct sunlight.

ANISE *(Pimpinella anisum)* An annual that grows to a height of 24 inches, anise can be planted as soon as all danger of frost is passed. Because seedlings do not transplant well, sow seeds directly in the container or pot. Provide plenty of sun. When flower clusters turn gray-brown, collect seeds by clipping into a paper bag. Store dried seeds in airtight containers protected from bright light.

BASIL, SWEET *(Ocimum basilicum)* One of the more popular annuals, basil reaches a height of 24 inches at maturity. Usually started from seed indoors 6 to 8 weeks before outdoor sowing. When seedlings are established, harden off by placing outside during the day. Then transplant to a container that gets plenty of sun. Keep plants pinched back for more vigorous growth. To harvest, pinch the leaves off the stem and spread out in a well-ventilated shady area until dry. Store dried leaves in airtight containers and out of bright light.

BAY *(Laurus nobilis)* Perennial. Grows from 3 to 6 feet tall in a tub or pot, but in its native Mediterranean area, trees have reached 60 feet in height. Because growth from a seed or from cuttings takes months, buy small plants from a nursery or garden supply center. The plants require some sun and well-drained soil. In southern regions, small clusters of yellow flowers often appear. Bay is primarily an ornamental tree, but fresh or dried leaves can be used in cooking. To dry the leaves, hang branches in a dark room where the temperature never gets above 70 degrees Fahrenheit. When the leaves are just dry, spread each one flat between two cloths and weight down to flatten. Store in an airtight container. The plant will stand the first frost, but must winter inside in cold climates. Bay needs morning or afternoon sun and does best with cool 60-degree nights, good drainage, and fairly high humidity. Indoors,

place potted bay plants near a southern or eastern window. Mist occasionally, and water when soil surface feels dry.

BORAGE *(Borago officinalis)* An annual that grows to about 18 inches in height, borage is sown from seed in early spring. Plants produce handsome, starlike blue or white blossoms in early summer and continue blooming until fall. Blossoms are especially attractive to bees. Keep in sunny location. Harvest young leaves as needed. Blossoms can be used as garnishes for beverages.

CARAWAY *(Carum carvi)* Biennial. Grows to 8 inches tall the first year and up to 24 inches the second. Sow seeds in a sunny location in late fall or early spring. After flower clusters turn brown, clip into a paper bag. Store seeds in an airtight container.

CATNIP *(Nepeta cataria)* Perennial grows up to 36 inches high. Plant seeds or divisions in fall or early spring. Thrives in full sun or partial shade and will spread rapidly. To harvest, pinch the leaves off and spread in a well-ventilated area until dry to the touch. Store dried leaves in an airtight container away from bright light.

CHERVIL *(Anthriscus cerefolium)* Often growing to a height of 24 inches, chervil can be planted in a sunny location in late fall or early spring. Be sure seeds aren't buried too deeply because exposure to light is required for good germination. Keep plants pinched back for more vigorous growth. Leaves may be picked as needed. To harvest, clip whole plant before flowering and hang upside down in a shady, well-ventilated place. Store dried leaves in an airtight container kept in a dark room or cupboard. For winter chervil, simply move pot or container indoors or resow.

CHIVES *(Allium schoenoprasum)* Coveted not only for its subtle onion flavor, but also for its globular lavender blossoms, chives grow up to 12 inches tall. Plant seeds or divisions in early spring in a sunny

location. Pinch back occasionally to encourage bushier growth. Pick leaves at any time by cutting at base of plant. Best to use leaves immediately because flavor diminishes as leaves dry out. Leaves may be frozen for future use. Divide plants every few years to prevent crowding and loss of vigor. For winter harvest, pot up a clump or two for the kitchen window. Garlic chives grow taller and have garlic-flavored foliage and delicate, white blossoms.

COMFREY *(Symphytum officinale)* A perennial that grows as high as 30 inches, comfrey is usually grown from seeds or divisions. Reserve a sunny location, and mix lime with the soil for a slightly alkaline level. Pick entire plant just before flowers open. Spread leaves and roots in a well-ventilated, sunny area until dry. Store in airtight containers. Fresh young leaves may be used in salads or tea.

CORIANDER *(Coriandrum sativum)* Annual. Grows to 30 inches high. Plant outdoors in a sunny location after all danger of frost has passed. Because seedlings are difficult to transplant, sow seeds where plants are to remain. When the flower clusters turn brown, harvest the seeds by clipping into a paper bag.

CRESS *(Lepidium sativum)* Annual that grows up to 12 inches high. Also known as pepper grass, garden cress should not be confused with watercress, which is a member of the nasturtium family. Cress is an early spring, quick crop often used in salads or as an attractive garnish. Sow seeds thickly in the spring as soon as the container soil can be worked. Because plants germinate and grow rapidly, plan on successive sowings every 10 to 14 days for a continuous crop. Cress also can be grown indoors in pots on a sunny windowsill for an all-winter harvest. Leaves can be harvested as early as 10 days after planting. Cress also can be grown for its tasty sprouts. Several forms are sold for garden use, but the most popular are the curled-leaved varieties.

DILL (*Anethum graveolens*) An annual that grows to a height of 36 inches, dill is planted in a sunny location as soon as all danger of frost has passed. To harvest leaves, pinch off in early summer and quick-dry in a cool, airy place. Seal dried leaves in an airtight container as quickly as possible. When flower heads turn brown, harvest the seeds by snipping umbels into a paper bag. Store seeds in an airtight container.

FENNEL (*Foeniculum vulgare*) Annual; perennial in warmer regions. Reaching a height of 4 feet, fennel can be planted after all danger of frost is passed. Fresh leaves may be used as they mature. When flower heads have turned brown, harvest seeds by clipping the seed umbel into a paper bag.

GARLIC (*Allium sativum*) Perennial. Grows up to 24 inches high. May be planted as soon as the soil can be worked. In late summer when the tops begin to turn yellow, bend them over with the back of a

rake. Dig the cloves when the foliage has turned completely brown. Store bulbs in a net bag, or braid the tops together to form a garlic "rope." Hang bags and ropes in a cool, dark, well-ventilated place.

GERANIUM, SCENTED (*Pelargonium* sp.) Treated as an annual in colder regions, scented geraniums can grow up to 2 feet in height. There are over 75 varieties with scented leaves, usually divided into six categories: rose, lemon, mint, fruit, spice, and pungent. Start seeds indoors 10 to 12 weeks before outdoor planting, or buy established seedlings. Transplant to container after all danger of frost has passed. Ideal for hanging baskets, the leaves can be picked as needed. For drying, cut leaves in the fall and dry in a well-ventilated, shady area. Store in airtight containers or use in nosegays, potpourris, and sachets.

HOREHOUND (*Marrubium vulgare*) Perennial that grows from 1 to 3 feet high. Start from seeds in spring or fall, then propagate with

cuttings in spring through summer. Or divide large plants in the spring. Set plants about 1 foot apart in full sun. Horehound does well in poor, dry soil; cut plants back during growth to avoid burr-like blossoms in June through September. Bees are attracted to the small, white flowers and will produce a uniquely flavored honey. The fresh leaves have a musky smell that is lost in drying. The fresh or dry leaves can be used to make tea or a syrup that can be used in candy or cough medicine. Dry leaves quickly by hanging in bunches in a warm location. Then seal the dried leaves in an airtight container. Plants may be potted and brought indoors as kitchen window plants.

LAVENDER (*Lavandula* sp.) Perennial. Grows to 32 inches high. Three varieties are commonly grown: English or true lavender is the showiest and produces the most fragrant flowers; spike lavender produces larger, more fragrant leaves; and French lavender is grown as a bath fragrance. Start seeds of all varieties indoors 10 to 12 weeks before outside planting. Sow extra seeds to make up for losses due to low germination rates. After all danger of frost is passed, plant seedlings outdoors in a container that gets ample sun. Harvest fresh leaves as needed and flower heads before they open. If lavender is to stay outdoors through the winter, protect with a 2- or 3-inch layer of mulching material.

LEMON BALM (*Melissa officinalis*) A perennial that grows to about 24 inches in height, lemon balm is usually started indoors 10 to 12 weeks before outdoor planting so you can enjoy an early crop. Seeds can be sown outdoors as soon as the soil is workable. Because exposure to light is required for germination, seeds should not be covered completely. Harvest fresh leaves as needed.

LEMON VERBENA (*Aloysia triphylla*) A perennial reaching heights of 6 feet or more, lemon verbena is planted after danger of frost has passed. Purchase healthy, established plants from a nursery or

Winter usually spells doom for plants, but not for this windowsill herb garden. A southern exposure offers the perfect setting for sun-loving herbs. The location is also handy for harvesting, to spice up your cooking and to garnish meals. The jars hold fresh herb jellies; the jug and bottle contain herb vinegars.

garden center for immediate planting. As fall approaches, lemon verbena will drop its leaves. It can be stored in a cold frame or cellar. Use leaves as needed, or quick dry by spreading out on trays in a cool, shady place. Store in an airtight container. Excellent for use in potpourris or to flavor drinks and stuffings.

MARJORAM (Origanum majorana) Planted as an annual in cooler areas but a perennial in warmer climates. Grows to 12 or more inches in height. Plant seeds indoors 8 to 10 weeks before outdoor planting time, then transplant to containers after all danger of frost has passed. For best results, place container in sunny location. After blossoms have faded, shear back entire plant several inches to encourage new growth. To harvest, hang plants in a warm, well-ventilated area until dry. Strip off leaves and store in an airtight container.

MINT (Mentha sp.) Perennial. The most common varieties are apple mint, orange mint, spearmint, and black peppermint. Height varies with variety but ranges anywhere between 12 and 36 inches. Plant seeds or root divisions in early spring, and divide every few years to keep the plants from becoming too crowded. Harvest fresh leaves at any time. To dry, cut back stems to the second set of leaves just before the plants are about to flower. Hang stems in a well-ventilated, shady place. Store in airtight containers out of bright light.

OREGANO (Origanum vulgare) A perennial that grows to heights of 12 inches, oregano can be planted from seed after all danger of frost has passed. Keep plants pinched back to encourage bushy growth. To harvest, clip off leaves as the plants begin to flower and dry in a sunny, well-ventilated area. Store in airtight containers. Cover plants with 2 or 3 inches of mulch, if pots are to be left in the open.

PARSLEY (Petroselinum crispum) Biennial. Grows to 12 inches in height. Seeds may be started outdoors as soon as soil is workable. Use leaves as they mature or dry by hanging pulled up plant in a shady, well-ventilated area. Crumble leaves and store in airtight bottles or plastic containers. To freeze, wash in several changes of water, then blanch in boiling water for ten seconds. Chill in ice water for a minute. Pat dry with paper toweling. Wrap and freeze. In late summer, pot up plants for a winter harvest.

ROSEMARY (Rosmarinus officinalis) A perennial in warm climates, rosemary will grow to a height of 4 feet. Start seeds indoors, or take stem cuttings and start in commercially prepared potting soil. Use leaves fresh. To dry, cut plant back by half while in bloom. Cure leaves in a well-ventilated, shady area. Store in airtight containers.

SAGE (Salvia officinalis) Perennial. Grows up to 30 inches high. Because considerable time is required for mature plants to develop, set out root divisions or stem cuttings. Use leaves fresh as needed. To dry, cut back the stem tips when the flower buds begin to form. Spread out in a well-ventilated, shady area.

SUMMERY SAVORY (Satureja hortensis) Annual. Summery Savory reaches heights of about 18 inches and produces dark green leaves and tiny white, pink, or lavender flowers. Sow seeds in early spring, and place container in a sunny location. To dry, cut the whole plant just before flowering and hang in a shady, well-ventilated place.

SWEET CICELY (Myrrhis odorata) A perennial 2 or 3 feet tall at maturity, sweet cicely is usually sown from seed so plant can be triggered by a freeze and thaw cycle. In spring, transplant seedlings or divide roots. Needs rich moist soil and shade. Anise-flavored leaves or seeds may be used. Roots can be eaten raw or cooked. If plants reach full maturity, they will re-seed themselves.

SWEET WOODRUFF (Galium odoratum) Perennial. An attractive ground cover that rarely exceeds 6 to 8 inches in height, sweet woodruff is a quick spreader. Because seeds are extremely slow in germinating, plant established seedlings purchased at a nursery or garden supply center. It's also possible to take stem cuttings. Give woodruff a shady location and somewhat acid soil. Once plants have taken hold, the woodruff bed will expand rapidly and require frequent pruning. Harvest leaves while the plant is in bloom, and dry in a shady, well-ventilated area. Leaves are especially useful for making "May Wine." Dry leaves have the odor of newly mown hay.

TARRAGON (artemisia dracunculus) Perennial. Grows to 30 inches high. Sow seeds or plant stem cuttings in a sunny location in early spring. When buying seeds, be sure to ask for the German or French varieties. The Russian type is much less tasty. Divide established beds every two or three years, and keep plants well mulched to protect the shallow root system. Use fresh leaves as needed. To dry, cut the plants back to a height of 4 inches in early summer and early fall. Spread out in a shady, well-ventilated place then store in airtight containers. If plants are to be left outdoors, provide a generous mulch at least 3 inches thick as protection against winter cold. Or, you can pot up young plants in late summer for a sunny windowsill. Keep soil moist.

THYME (Thymus vulgaris) A popular perennial, thyme is available in a number of varieties, some of which are erect growing, while others are compact and low growing. As a general rule, seeds are started 4 to 6 weeks before outdoor planting, or seedlings purchased from a nursery are set out. Use leaves fresh as needed. To dry, cut plants back to a height of 2 inches just before flowers begin to open and dry in a shady, well-ventilated area. After leaves have dried thoroughly, place in airtight containers away from direct light. Because thyme is attractive to bees, many gardeners like to locate plants near the vegetable garden to enhance pollination. In cold climates, protect plants with a thick layer of mulch in winter.

GREEN THUMB BASICS

POTS AND POTTING

By definition a container is confining. If plants are to thrive, therefore, it's important they get the right soil in the right amount over the right kind of drainage.

BASICS

Believe it or not, when you fill a pot with soil, you are actually launching a tiny environment teeming with bacteria, organic matter, moisture, minerals, and pore spaces. Water moves in and out, pulling in air as it goes. Nutrients play a chemical game with roots that exchange useless ions for food ions. And bacteria, constantly foraging for food, break down organic matter into a form plants can use effectively.

POTS

There are practically as many different kinds of pots as there are plants that go into them. The range includes monstrous wooden tubs capable of supporting a small forest all the way down to the lilliputian "thumb" pots which, as the name suggests, can accommodate a thumb, green or otherwise. The materials vary, too. With advances in technology have come synthetic materials, most of which can be coaxed into a variety of containers.

For a pot, however, the main requirement is that it hold soil. Next in importance is drainage. No matter what you grow, with the exception of water plants, most things with roots won't tolerate a soggy, continually wet soil. When shopping, be sure a prospective container has some provision for drainage. Depending on what the pot is made of, most will have a single hole in the bottom where excess water can drain off.

CLAY Because of its capacity to "breathe," that is, allow moisture and air to penetrate, clay is still the favorite among the gardening elite. In addition to its porous structure, clay also offers visual attraction. Who can resist the quaint texture of an heirloom pot covered with centuries of earthy stains? At the same time, the rich brick-red color acts as a perfect setting for plant foliage. But there are disadvantages, too. They can become heavy, and they break easily. Also, a clay pot, if not presoaked for several hours before using, will soak up soil moisture and leave a newly potted plant high and dry.

PLASTIC Not since Linnaeus decided to classify plants has anything affected the home gardener so much as the introduction of the plastic pot. Light in weight, non-breakable, and easy to transport, plastic is the clear favorite among nurserymen—not to mention many a person whose hobby is gardening. Like it or not, the plastic pot is a fact of horticultural life,

and although it may lack some of the class of clay, it has some very definite advantages. To begin with, plastic pots are easy to work with. Drop one and it will bounce back hardly the worse for wear. Their light weight makes them easy to store. And they are inexpensive. Finally, the imperviousness of plastic can be an asset, if understood and turned into an advantage instead of a liability.

WOOD For attractiveness and sheer practicality, few materials measure up to wood. Best of all, wood offers all kinds of creative possibilities for the do-it-yourselfer who has hankered to try pot making. Almost anything handy will do for wood, if proper preservation steps are taken. The best wood by far is redwood or cypress, because both naturally resist rotting. Be sure to use waterproof glue and galvanized, brass, or aluminum nails or screws for longer life. Screws are recommended because they can be adjusted to the shrinkage or expansion of the wood.

For the patio, deck, and balcony owner, wood is ideal because containers can be custom built to fit snugly into nooks and crannies. A neglected corner, for example, can become a wonderland of cascading flowers by building a special triangular planter. Or try a modular concept and build a set of boxes that can be stacked, placed in tandem, or scattered about to suit your every design need or changing fancy.

MISCELLANEOUS Then there is that peculiar ceramic jug rescued from grandma's attic or that large cast iron kettle dragged home from a neighborhood sale. These may be superb containers, but don't forget drainage. You simply have to find a way to allow water to escape so your prize plant doesn't become a heap of wilted leaves. With time and patience, you can drill holes, or if the container is large enough, simply fill the bottom with plenty of gravel or small stones and set a plastic or clay pot inside. Old pros at the potting game often plant directly into the container, insisting that excess water will collect below the gravel. This is risky for the beginning container grower because the margin for error is narrow.

SOIL

Pots, whether ornamental or functional, have to do with appearance. With soil, however, we come to the meat of the matter, because the failure or success of a choice plant depends on the home its roots get.

There are three main reasons for soil: 1. soil provides a means of physical support so the plant can stand upright for greatest exposure to the sun; 2. a medium in which roots can grow and seek out plant food; and 3. soil provides a storehouse where air, water, and essential nutrients can come and go freely. Once these factors are present, plants will quickly take hold and thrive.

What you use for soil depends largely on what you intend to grow. But the problem is complicated somewhat by the fact that containers may be shifted from time to time, suspended from wire, attached to a windowsill, or simply plunked down in one spot to remain forever. As a result, weight becomes a crucial factor. Here are two basic mixes, a heavyweight for light pots and permanent tubs and a lightweight for hanging baskets, windowboxes, and heavy pots.

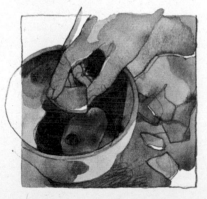

HEAVYWEIGHT (all purpose)
    1 part garden loam
    1 part sphagnum peat moss
    1 part coarse sand
LIGHTWEIGHT
    1 part garden loam
    1 part sphagnum peat moss
    1 part perlite or vermiculite

Remember, too, that some plants are heavy feeders while others can subsist on the barest minimum. Vegetables, for example, will respond to supplemental doses of dried cow manure or commercial fertilizers. Herbs on the other hand aren't too fussy, while nasturtiums will produce all leaves and few flowers if fed too generously.

HOW TO POT

In a burst of generosity, some gardeners will shoot the works on soil, figuring it's free. Trouble is, a seedling plant plunged into a huge tub of soil will make a mad dash to fill up all that space with roots. Consequently, leaves and stems will be neglected, while flowers will be slow in appearing—if they appear at all. The trick is to match plant and pot so roots get just what they need, no more, no less. In general, a new pot should be about one inch larger than the plant's former pot. It seems like scrimping, but roots take time to expand into their new quarters. If you are starting cuttings or offshoots, a three- or four-inch pot is sufficient. Then simply follow these basic steps:

DRAINAGE Check pot to be sure there is a drainage hole or holes. Then cover bottom with an inch (two inches for large containers) of broken crockery or small stones. Place a layer of sphagnum peat moss over drainage material to prevent soil from sifting through.

REMOVING PLANT Gently knock plant out of its old pot by cradling plant and soil in one hand and tapping the rim of the pot against a table edge with the other hand. Take care to keep as much of the root ball intact as possible.

TRANSFER Place plant in the center of the new pot, making sure old soil level (visible on stem) is at least one inch below the pot's rim. Fill remaining space with soil and firm around roots.

WATER Water well so soil settles in and around roots. Keep plant out of direct sunlight for a day or two before returning to its accustomed spot. This rest helps the plant adjust from the shock of transplanting.

REPOTTING

Eventually, a plant's ever-expanding roots will bump into container sides. But growth doesn't stop. Roots will wind around and around in a futile search for unoccupied territory. Left unchecked, the plant will wrap itself into a tangled mess and begin to wither. When this happens, it's time to repot. If you're unsure about root conditions, remove plant from pot and inspect. If you find a wall of interwoven roots exactly matching the inside shape of the pot, the plant is rootbound. Simply repot in a new, slightly larger container. A thorough watering beforehand will help separate roots from pot and preserve the root ball. To repot extra large plants, lay the pot on its side and split the container open.

GREEN THUMB BASICS

WATERING

More plants die because of overwatering than from any other single cause. When roots become waterlogged from overwatering, the plant literally drowns.

OVERWATERING

Perhaps it's the commuter life that inspires gardeners to undertake their watering chores with production line efficiency. Whatever the cause, plants are often dunked whether they need it or not. What is seldom understood is that roots need to "breathe" to carry on their function of absorbing nutrients and, at the same time, expelling waste materials.

The two coleus above were the same size and shape when potted. The one on the left was watered only when the soil surface started to dry. The other received daily soakings, with the result that some leaves lost their luster, others dropped, and growth was stunted.

The problem is there are just too many variables affecting when and how much to water. For example, a warm, dry house will practically pull moisture from soil and leaves. A pot suspended near the ceiling will suffer temperatures several degrees higher than plants on the floor. The kind of pot makes a difference, too. Porous clay allows water to penetrate and eventually evaporate, while plastic

holds water in. Or a plant may be in direct sun or near a source of heat. Clouds may block the sun for days, reducing moisture loss. On the other hand, a brisk wind sweeping across a patio or deck may dry out containers. Humidity is a factor as well. On wet, muggy days water evaporation slows, while on dry, hot days evaporation is high. Then there are the habits of the plants themselves to consider. Some, like the succulents, are accustomed to dry, arid conditions, while African violets show a preference for soggy, tropical soils.

The point is, watering should not be a mindless task undertaken with robot-like precision. You have to water according to each plant's needs, and those needs will vary. As you make the rounds of your container garden, touch the soil as you go. If the surface to a depth of an inch or so feels dry, then reach for the watering can. Wilting also means water is scarce. But don't panic. Plants bounce back quickly, even

though drooping leaves look doomed. Once you have become an old pro at watering, you can sometimes tell how much water is in the soil by the sound produced when a pot is rapped with the knuckles.

WHEN TO WATER

Schedule your waterings during the morning hours so plants can dry off thoroughly before sunset. Wet plants exposed to cooler nighttime temperatures are good candidates for disease. Watering in the morning also means plants get moisture during daylight hours when optimum growth occurs. If night watering is unavoidable, apply water at base of plant so leaves remain dry.

Daily, mist foliage of ferns and other plants that thrive in high humidity. Misting in the morning will allow the plants to dry off completely during the day, rather than stand damp overnight.

On bright, sunny days, the loss of water through evaporation and plant transpiration is much greater than on cloudy days. Be prepared to increase waterings on bright days and hold back a little on gloomy, overcast days.

HOW MUCH WATER

Adjust watering amounts to fit the structure of the soil. Sandy soil does not retain moisture well, which means water will have to be added at more frequent intervals. A rich, humusy soil, on the other hand, is almost sponge-like in its ability to soak up and hold water.

When wielding the watering can, keep in mind that plants would rather have too little water than too much. Roots stuck in a swampy container soil will, believe it or not, suffocate. Once you do decide moisture is needed, don't be timid. It's much better to thoroughly drench a plant once a week than offer a trickle every day. When water seeps out of the bottom into a saucer or onto the terrace, the soil is thoroughly saturated. Dump the saucer or tray so pot doesn't sit in water. If your antique

jardiniere has no drainage hole but simply houses a plant potted in clay or plastic, remove the plant periodically to drain excess water from the decorator pot.

Smaller pots can be given a dunking every month or two. Fill a sink or tub with water deep enough so the water is just above the rim of the pot. Set pot under water and leave until bubbling stops. Remove from water and allow to drain into saucer or sink. This is a good time to take stock of your plant's general health. Remove dead leaves and check for injurious insects.

During the winter months, cold water taken directly from the tap may be so cold it will shock roots into

temporary inactivity. Leaves will wilt, but plants will generally recover. Avoid root shock by simply mixing a little warm water with the cold. Or fill the watering can after your watering chores are completed, so the water is at room temperature the next time you begin your rounds. Ideal water temperature is around 60 degrees Fahrenheit.

CONSIDER THE POT

Be aware of what containers are made of and how the plant is potted. Plastic and ceramic pots lock in water, which means fewer waterings are necessary. Clay, however, absorbs water and thereby contributes to moisture loss through evaporation. Wood insulates and keeps soil temperatures even. As a result, moisture levels will not drop as quickly. Remember, too, that containers without drainage holes will obviously retain more water than a container shot through with holes.

If a garden hose is used, remember water is under considerable pressure, and a fair amount of soil may be splattered about by the force. Use a water breaker attachment to reduce the pressure of the water.

KNOW YOUR PLANTS

Read available literature, and talk to neighbors who are fellow gardeners. Although plants are collected in your living room, they have their distant roots in all parts of the world. As a result, the climate and soil they need differ. Learn which plants prefer the environment you can supply easily.

VACATION CARE

To be safe, don't leave plants on their own for more than two weeks. If you intend to be away longer, have a neighbor make the rounds with the watering can for you.

The first step is to move as many plants as possible out of direct sunshine; place them in a shady area. Containers too heavy to move may have to be shaded with a portable screen. If you go south during the winter, help plants survive your absence by turning down the heat to 60 or even 55 degrees Fahrenheit.

Remember, the smaller the pot, the quicker it will dry out. Construct miniature greenhouses out of plastic bags stapled at the top. Sticks pushed into the soil will prevent the bag from resting on leaves. Or if a container is large, wrap the tub right up to the plant stem with plastic. When watering, stick to normal amounts, so things don't get moldy inside the bags. Seal tightly, so moisture doesn't escape. Your plants will survive for at least two weeks.

Or devise a system of water-filled basins connected to pots by means of wicks. Place pots so bottoms are out of the water. Then insert wicks through drain holes. For the utmost in automatic watering, try the drip irrigation system using an elevated container filled with water and maybe a dash of a soluble fertilizer. Plastic tubing with a regulator clip attached carries a steady supply of liquid nourishment to the plant.

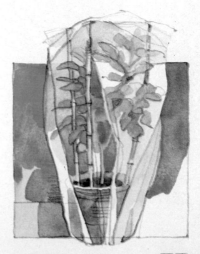

77

GREEN THUMB BASICS

FEEDING AND PEST PROBLEMS

All may look quiet on the garden front when you pause to take in the quiet beauty of plants. However, there's a world of activity deep inside the bulky containers.

IT'S A SMALL WORLD

Root hairs by the millions are creeping between soil particles in search of moisture and nutrients that can be shipped upstairs to growing

leaves and stems. Unfortunately, there are limits to the plant's small world. Ensconced in barely a bushel of soil, plants are also removed from a host of natural processes that tend to replenish the soil. Consequently, it's up to the container caretaker to see that food is made available at the right time and in the right amount.

HOW TO FEED

The big three nutrients most important to living plants are nitrogen, phosphorus, and potassium.

NITROGEN Helps leaf growth and is essential for chlorophyll formation, the magic green stuff that helps plants manufacture food.

PHOSPHORUS Important for flowering, fruiting, and root development.

POTASSIUM Contributes to strong stems and at the same time improves plants' resistance to disease. Calcium, magnesium, and sulfur are also important nutrients. So are a host of trace elements, such as iron, zinc, copper, boron, chlorine, and molybdenum. All are found in plants and are required for healthy development, even though scientists aren't sure how they all function.

Luckily for the home gardener, you don't have to be a whiz at chemistry to keep plants well fed. Scientists have isolated the substances needed for good growth, and garden supply manufacturers provide a variety of fertilizers that are effective and easy to use. And you have a choice. Fer-

tilizers are available in dry or wet forms. The dry is usually mixed with the potting soil before the plant is transplanted to the container. The wet form is dissolved in water and applied with a watering can or through a special attachment to the garden hose. Then there are the modern "slow-release" fertilizers consisting of coated granules that gradually release nutrients over an extended period. Check your garden center for the slow-release fertilizers now on the market. Wait until you are ready to plant, however, before mixing any of these fertilizers into the soil because contact with water will trigger the release process. Applied too early, most of the nutrients will be gone by the time plant roots occupy the soil. Or you can opt for strictly organic fertilizers, such as fish emulsion, bone meal, cottonseed meal, or dried blood, not to mention a wide variety of animal manures.

Whatever material you use, the package will almost always display a numerical code that will help you determine exactly what you are getting and in what amounts. For example, a soluble fertilizer might indicate an analysis of 15-30-15. The first number, regardless of who manufactures the fertilizer, indicates the percentage of nitrogen, the second number the percentage of phosphorus, and the last number the percentage of potassium. Reliable brands will also give you an idea of the trace elements present, as well as the amount of inert material included. Why all the mathematics? Because some plants differ in what they need and when they need it. For example, if you are fascinated with the idea of growing spinach or lettuce in your container garden, you'll want lush leafy growth and not a forest of useless blossom heads. So a fertilizer high in nitrogen is recommended, which means you should look for a high first number such as 16-0-0 (nitrate of soda).

There is a danger in all of this juggling of nutrients; it's tempting to flood everything in the garden with gallons of plant food. Overfeeding, however, can do considerable harm. Too much of a good thing can burn roots and stems or alter the growth cycle by encouraging plants to become full-time leaf producers at the expense of blossoms and fruits. Most experts recommend feedings once every two or three weeks. The best approach, though, is to become as familiar as you can with your plants and how they look when hungry, dried out, or generally under the weather. Eventually, you'll be able to fit your program to the exact needs of your plants.

Here are a handful of tips to keep in mind:

1. Make sure the soil is sufficiently moist before applying fertilizer. Applied to a dry soil, fertilizer can burn roots and stems.

2. Mix fertilizer at half strength for those plants that require less feeding, such as geraniums, nasturtium, and most herbs.

3. Do not fertilize dormant plants. Most growing things lapse into a period of inactivity when days shorten and nights lengthen. Once spring arrives and days get longer, plants renew growth and will welcome a taste of fertilizer.

4. Try not to overfertilize, because too much growth can produce weak stems and stalks, not to mention a forest of leaves.

5. Avoid the accumulation of salts (whitish deposits on soil and pot rims) by periodically leaching the soil. Drench pot with tepid water until excess runs out the bottom. If deposits are heavy, repeat two or three times every half hour.

DISEASES AND PESTS

Nothing is more inviting to insects than a container garden that has become a jungle of sickly, mold-infested plants. Poor ventilation, rank growth, overcrowding, and dead leaves are practically neon messages to insects that good eats and safe

quarters are near at hand. The best way to keep pests at bay is to keep plants healthy and unattractive to insects. Sometimes all that is needed to foil attackers are good gardening practices:

1. Keep containers, patio, and work area clean. After completing potting and fertilizing, wipe up spilled soil or liquid. When starting seeds or cuttings, use only sterilized soil to prevent the spread of fungus diseases. Old pots should be scrubbed and washed before using again.

2. Maintain a constant vigil for dead leaves and spent blossoms. Remove and destroy if infested. If a diseased plant appears doomed, remove immediately so remaining plants don't succumb.

3. Give plants plenty of elbow room to prevent overcrowding. One of the best ways to prevent disease is to provide good ventilation.

4. If an infested plant has no hope of survival, suppress your sentimental attachments and throw it out. A terminally ill plant is difficult, if not impossible, to revive and will only take surrounding plants with it.

5. At least once a year give the garden area a thorough housecleaning.

Not every problem caused by insects warrants a battery of devastating sprays or chemicals. Most can be easily controlled if detected early enough by simply spraying with water or by dunking the affected plant in a mild soap bath. If these initial methods fail, use an organically derived pesticide, such as rotenone or pyrethrum. Both are nonresidual and relatively safe to use. For isolated problems, a pest strip or two placed near suffering plants can provide all the control you need. When specific

insects threaten, follow these simple remedies:

APHIDS Small, soft-bodied insects that cluster on the undersides of leaves and near tender leaf and flower buds, aphids can be discouraged by spraying the plant with a forceful stream of water. Or dunk the plant gently into a tub of soapy water. For severe infestations, spray plants, especially undersides of leaves, with rotenone or pyrethrum.

WHITE FLY A telltale sign of attack by this insect is a cloud of white specks that appears when the plant is disturbed. Fuchsia, geranium, basil, coleus, and tomato are some of the plants susceptible. Rotenone or malathion, if used regularly, will provide effective control.

SPIDER MITES Difficult to see because of their small size, mites can be detected by the presence of wispy webs often located at leaf axils. Thorough control is chancy at best. Because spider mites thrive in a desert-dry environment, mist plant foliage daily to discourage the critters from taking up lodgings. Sometimes best to dispose of plant. Ivies are especially susceptible. If spraying is unavoidable, use a special miticide designed for the purpose.

MEALY BUGS The appearance of cotton-like clumps on flower stems or in leaf axils is a sure sign that mealy bugs are present. Malathion works effectively.

SCALE Another in the rogues' gallery of sucking pests, scale insects are especially attracted to ferns and citrus plants. Young scale are small and difficult to detect until hard, brown shells become visible. Remove with a soft toothbrush or wet cloth.

Keep in mind, though, that just because a plant appears languid and out of sorts doesn't necessarily mean insects are the cause. In many cases, poor cultural practices are to blame. Before reaching for the nearest spray, inspect the plant carefully to identify the trouble.

GREEN THUMB BASICS

PROPAGATION

Half the joy of gardening is watching the miracle of propagation firsthand. Each cell of a plant has locked within it, the astounding capacity to re-create the original type of flora.

IT'S EASY

If you are especially fond of a particular specimen, simply snip off a few sprigs, plunk them in moist sand, and in no time you'll have dozens of look alikes ready for transplanting. Or collect the seeds and sow as many as your house and yard will hold. Bend a stem and pin it to the soil; soon tiny, pale white roots will spring into action. Roots, bulbs, leaves, and stems also have the power to trigger growth.

Every gardener has sown a packet of seeds, but not everyone has tried a

softwood cutting or attempted air layering. Seeds are by far the most common form of propagation. But cuttings, whether from stem, root, or leaf, require considerably less time and, best of all, are free for the taking.

There are other good reasons for propagating your plants. Growing things know no bounds when it comes to filling the spaces allotted to them. Asparagus fern, for example, will droop and sprawl in every direction until the gardener intervenes to halt its rank progress. Once over-

grown, most plants will take on a slightly yellow tinge and appear positively unkempt. Make the rounds and put the brakes on plants that are gradually outproducing their roots.

How you keep your container plants in check depends on what you are growing and where. Some plants, such as iris and peonies, can be dug up and divided. Most of the bulb varieties are also kept in bounds by division. Other plants need to be snipped and pruned to encourage fuller growth and more abundant blossoms. And each of the cuttings, of course, can be made to produce a new plant.

Whatever the plant, it's important that the proper conditions are provided for successful propagation. Fortunately, little equipment is needed. All you need is a supply of sand, flowerpots or seed flats, and a square foot or so of plastic film. It also helps to have a quantity of sphagnum moss, some twine, a sharp knife or razor blade, and rooting powder on hand. If you have a smattering of the scientist in you, then try putting together a special propagating frame. All you need is a wood frame and a glass or plastic top to keep in the moisture. Or you can reclaim an old terrarium for your propagating project.

As for soil, the important thing is that it be sterile. If sand is used, avoid the chance of disease by flushing with boiling water. The synthetic soils, such as perlite and vermiculite, are already sterile and may be used

as is. Remember, to grow things is ultimately a personal and creative project. So don't hesitate to dabble in different techniques and even devise some of your own. For example, you might want to experiment with the cutting medium; try mixing various proportions of sphagnum, peat moss, vermiculite, perlite, and sand to see what works best for you and your plants.

ROOT DIVISION

Root division is clearly the easiest way to propagate those plants that grow in clumps, such as Boston fern, peony, iris, peperomia, and most of the herbs.

To ease the shock to plants, be sure to water thoroughly a day or so before you plan to divide. Then, turn the pot or container upside down, supporting the plant and root ball with one hand. Tap the pot rim on a table or other wooden surface to loosen the root ball. The plant should slip easily from its container. Shake excess soil from the roots so you can determine the best place to make the division.

Generally, you can pull the plant in

half by gently pulling it apart. But occasionally, the roots are tough and hopelessly tangled. If it's rootbound, use a sharp knife to cut the sections apart. It may sound like cruel and unjust treatment, considering the plant has only sprouted a twig or two too many, but individual divisions will bounce right back if you pot them up quickly.

Water the new plants daily for at least a week, and keep them out of direct sunlight for about two weeks to give them time to initiate new root growth in their fresh soil.

CUTTINGS

The most common way to propagate is by taking soft wood cuttings. Although most will root fairly easily in water, water-grown roots tend to be brittle and may break off when potting more often than roots started in sand or perlite.

To take a soft wood cutting, cut off a four- to six-inch growing tip with a sharp knife or pruning shears. Make the cut at a 45-degree angle just below the point where a leaf joins the stem. Roots are most likely to form at these spots (known as leaf nodes).

Remove the lower leaves so the bottom two inches of stem are bare. If leaves are left on, they might rot and cause the cutting to die. Dip the cut end in a root-promoting powder to speed propagation. Insert the cutting in a container of moist, coarse sand or a mix of perlite and sphagnum peat moss. Water, and keep under a plastic wrap to prevent excess evaporation of moisture. If you use a plastic bag, place sticks in container to keep the plastic from touching the cuttings. If plants dry out, mist lightly

with a hand mister.

After three or four weeks, gently remove a cutting to check for roots. Pot up plants when roots have formed.

AIR LAYERING

Some large plants with woody stems drop their lower leaves if they get too little light or too much water. To revitalize the original plant and to propagate a new one, try air layering.

Simply make a cut part way through the stem at a severe angle, and insert a wooden match or toothpick to keep the cut open. Mold a wad of wet sphagnum moss the size of a baseball around the cut, enclose in a sheet of plastic, and tie at top and bottom. Make sure wrapping is as airtight as possible. Then keep the moss moist. In four weeks, the moss ball will be lined with new roots that will be visible through the plastic. Cut off the stem below the layering bag, and pot up after removing the plastic and twine. Shorten the remaining stem to three or four inches, and continue to water the old potted roots. New growth will sprout from the stub, and the plant will be revitalized.

RUNNERS & OFFSETS

Plants that send out aerial runners and form new plantlets are among the easiest to propagate. In their natural settings, these developing plantlets continue to descend until they come in contact with the moist forest floor. The young plants produce roots on contact and eventually become independent plants. When

grown at home, all you have to do is imitate this process. Fill a pot with soil and place the plantlet on top. When roots have taken hold, snip the runner leading to the parent plant. To start soil, use a mixture consisting of equal parts of sphagnum peat moss and coarse sand. Keep the starting medium moist. If the plant refuses to stay in one spot, pin it down with a hairpin or bent loop of wire. New roots should form in about four to five weeks. A good way to determine whether or not roots have formed is to gently feel the bottom of the plant. It should be anchored to the soil. Or you can give it a gentle tug or two. If it holds fast to the soil, it's ready for a life of its own.

LEAF CUTTINGS

African violet, gloxinias, and a number of begonia produce leaves that are capable of starting roots. Simply place leaves in water until tiny roots at least a quarter inch long have formed. Then transplant the young plants to small pots.

Another way to coax leaves into forming roots is to use coarse sand or a mixture of perlite and sphagnum peat moss. Simply insert leaf stems into the medium after it has been thoroughly moistened. Then water again to settle soil particles. Check for root formation after three or four weeks. An excellent way to supply the high humidity leaf cuttings like is to use a seed flat or even a plastic refrigerator box. Wrap the flat in plastic film, and check periodically to make certain sand doesn't dry out. Sometimes too much moisture will allow fungus to form. Ventilate cuttings if necessary.

GREEN THUMB BASICS

GROWING UNDER LIGHTS

Light, as everyone knows, is indispensable to growing things. But it doesn't always have to be sunlight. Try an artificial, cloudless setting if natural light is not available.

LIGHT FACTS

Not everyone lives under an unobstructed dome of clear blue sky, where a bright sun shines for days on end. In cities, high-rise buildings loom like cement clouds, shrouding the apartment dweller in darkness. Trees and foundation plants have crowded the windows so only a glimmer of sun sneaks through each day. Or perhaps it's a simple matter of the direction the home faces.

If you're insulated from the sun, your home doesn't have to be with-

out green things. Some plants, in fact, seem to prefer the cool or warm rays emitted by fluorescent tubes. Plan on a light garden in your cellar, or incorporate one into your living room design. Search your house for unused closets or for an empty, wasted space under a cabinet or a blank wall. By building light shelves or even a plant bench on wheels, you

can have things growing nearly anywhere. All you need is a fluorescent fixture and an electrical outlet.

A word about light and what it does for plants. Sunlight is actually a blend of different colors. We can see a hint of the color spectrum every time rain and sun meet to produce a rainbow. But there is more than meets the eye, because all we see is a narrow band at the center of the spectrum. Plants, though, can "see" the rays at the extreme ends, including ultraviolet and the far red wave lengths. In fact, scientists have discovered that far red light affects the number and frequency of blossoms, and that ultraviolet rays trigger growth of foliage. Light also plays a central role in the three important processes listed below.

PHOTOSYNTHESIS One of the reasons plants are like nothing else under the sun is their ability to produce their own food. All other living things depend on external sources and must either eat other animals or plants. How do plants do it? By combining carbon dioxide and water in the presence of light, they manufacture various carbohydrates to be stored for future use or consumed right away. No matter how much abuse a certain plant can take, it's got to have some light, whether direct or indirect, to carry on photosynthesis.

PHOTOPERIODISM Even more fascinating is that plants are sensitive to the absence and presence of light and dark, so much so they can be grouped according to their preferences. Long-day plants need extended periods of light, while short-day plants like abundant darkness and less light. A third group, which includes African violets, is indifferent to light quotas. In many cases,

whether or not a plant breaks into flower hinges on how much light it gets and when. Light at the wrong time may even cause certain plants *not* to bloom.

PHOTOTROPISM Then there is the peculiar hormone, auxin, found in the tender growing tips of plants. It will cause the plant to bend either toward or away from light. This tendency can become a handy signal to the home grower that conditions might be somewhat below par. A hunched, compact plant growing low to the pot is probably getting too much light, while tall, leggy growth with leaves separated by long, spindly stems is getting too little.

Of course, odd facts stumbled upon in a laboratory aren't always relevant when it comes to what's going on in the living room or cellar. But a vague idea of what light does and why plants need it will make it easier to build your own light garden, as well as effectively manipulate conditions so your plants will flourish.

EQUIPMENT

When it comes to putting together a light garden you can be as elaborate as your tools and talents will allow. Or you can in a matter of hours construct the "A" frame plant table, shown below, just to get things going. Keep these facts in mind, though, when you sit down to draw up your light garden plans:

1. Whenever possible, combine artificial light and available sunlight. If you can place your plants near a window, they will like it all the better.

2. Remember light intensity is important. For maximum light, place plants three to four inches from fluorescent bulbs. Because fluorescent bulbs maintain a low temperature, foliage is safe. Transformers, however, can give off heat. If you plan on an enclosed plant cabinet, allow some means of ventilation.

3. A wide variety of fluorescent bulbs are available. Some manufacturers have researched plant needs and produced specially designed grow bulbs. To get off on the right foot, equip your fixtures with these bulbs. However, studies have shown that cool white, warm white, and daylight bulbs in combination can be just as effective. Keep in mind, too, that fluorescent tubes begin to decline in light intensity after so many hours of use. As a general rule, most should be replaced after every 12 to 14 months of use. To keep track of when bulbs have been installed, simply write the date of installation on the end of the tube.

4. For most plants, you can figure on a minimum of 20 watts of fluorescent light per square foot of growing area. And don't forget you can increase the efficiency of fixtures by using reflectors to throw light back onto plant foliage. Even a simple white wall or white board along the back of the unit will reflect light onto the plants. When you buy a fixture, be sure a top reflector is included so you get the most from your bulbs. Fashion your own reflector if need be.

TIMING

The duration of light is critical, so plan on connecting an inexpensive timer to your fluorescent fixtures. Generally, you should allow 14 to 16 hours of light per day. For some plants, you might have to reduce this amount to about 12 hours for two months in the fall to trigger dormancy. In that case, you might consider grouping like plants and using different timers for the different time requirement.

TROUBLE SIGNS

A plant, more often than not, can give you valuable clues if it's in distress. If leaves appear yellow or become excessively compact, the chances are the light is too intense. Simply raise the fixture or move plants away. Few blossoms and deep green foliage, on the other hand, mean too little light. Try to keep humidity to between 40 and 60 per cent and temperature around 60 degrees Fahrenheit at night and 70 degrees during the day. Higher temperatures retard some plants' growth.

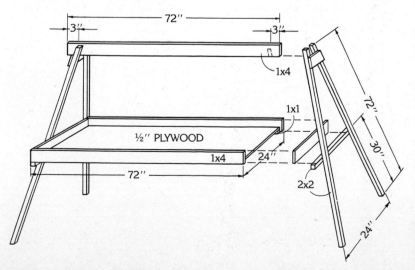

Favorite Indoor Plants

Houseplants are probably the first thing that comes to mind when you think of plants grown in containers. Unlike most container plants, many houseplants cannot survive outdoors year-round. And once inside, they need you to provide the care they receive naturally in their native home. How well they survive depends a great deal on how wisely they've been chosen. An amazing diversity of houseplants is available, and new varieties are being introduced yearly. With so many plants to choose from, selection is often difficult. Here are some factors to take into consideration.

The most important factor when buying a plant is the intensity of light it needs and how much you have to give it. You can adjust to a temperamental feeding or watering schedule, but there's little you can do about lack of light (if you object to using grow lights). Stick with lower-light plants.

Purchase healthy, well-shaped plants rather than those that are larger, but not as well formed. Occasionally, you can find some bargains among plants that have become overgrown, but be wary of any plant that looks sickly. Unless you're truly a cultural expert, you won't know what has made the plant unhealthy—or what to do to restore its health.

If you're a low-maintenance gardener, don't buy prima donna houseplants requiring much care.

Finally, certain homes are simply more suited to plants than others. Large windows, white walls, and lots of space to spare are features tailor-made for plants. But you can make do with less; install an artificial light unit, purchase a good room humidifier, or rearrange the furniture to provide window space. If you are truly interested in a particular plant, it's worth the time and effort to create a hospitable environment for it.

To ensure that all your indoor plants get the proper attention, the special charts provide all the cultural information you need at a glance. Proper light, correct watering, and propagation methods are included, plus comments that are of particular importance. Plants have been listed by their most widely known name, be it a common or a botanical name. Other nicknames have also been listed where appropriate.

🌿 FAVORITE INDOOR PLANTS 🌿

COMMON NAME	LIGHT	WATER	PROPAGATION	COMMENTS
African violet (*Saintpaulia* sp.)	Bright indirect	Water well when surface dries	Leaf cuttings or division	Likes porous soil high in humus
Airplane plant (*Chlorophytum comosum*) nickname: spider plant	Bright indirect	Water well when surface dries	Runners or division	Remove offsets to obtain new plants
Aralia (*Polyscias balfouriana*)	Sunny, bright indirect, or filtered	Evenly moist soil	Stem cuttings	Re-pot rootbound plants in spring
Asparagus ferns (*Asparagus meyeri*) (*Asparagus plumosus*) (*Asparagus sprengeri*)	Filtered	Evenly moist soil	Division	Mist foliage daily; asparagus fern is one of the hardiest ferns you can grow
Aspidistra (*Aspidistra elatior*) nickname: cast-iron plant	Bright indirect or filtered	Water well when surface dries	Division	Trim off brown leaf tips with scissors
Aucuba (*Aucuba japonica*)	Bright indirect	Evenly moist soil	Stem cuttings	Female produces red berries and purple flowers
Azalea (*Rhododendron* sp.)	Sunny or bright indirect	Evenly moist soil	Stem cuttings	Likes acid soil
Baby's-tears (*Soleirolia* sp. or *Nertera* sp.)	Filtered	Evenly moist soil	Stem cuttings or division	Likes soil high in humus
Bougainvillea (*Bougainvillea glabra*)	Sunny	Water well when surface dries	Stem cuttings	Blooms from late winter through summer
Brassaia (*Brassaia actinophylla*) nickname: schefflera	Bright indirect	Water well when surface dries	Air layering	Will attain ceiling height eventually; grows fairly slowly
Begonias: Rex begonias Tuberous begonias Wax begonias	Bright indirect Bright indirect Bright indirect	Evenly moist soil Evenly moist soil Evenly moist soil	Leaf cuttings Stem cuttings	Start tuberous begonias from tubers in February or March
Bromeliads	Bright indirect	Keep on dry side	Pot up offsets	Keep water in center cups
Chinese evergreen (*Aglaonema commutatum*)	Bright indirect or filtered	Evenly moist soil	Stem cuttings or division	Variegated types need medium to bright light
Christmas cactus (*Schlumbergera bridgesi*)	Bright indirect	Water well when surface dries	Stem cuttings	Withhold water in fall; keep in a cool place
Citrus trees	Sunny	Water well when surface dries	Grow from seeds	Mist foliage daily
Clivia (*Clivia miniata*)	Bright indirect	Evenly moist soil	Division	Reduce watering in winter

FAVORITE INDOOR PLANTS

COMMON NAME	LIGHT	WATER	PROPAGATION	COMMENTS
Coleus	Sunny or bright indirect	Evenly moist soil	Stem cuttings	Pinch tops to induce dense growth
Croton (*Codiaeum* sp.)	Sunny or bright indirect	Evenly moist soil	Air layering or stem cutting	Mist foliage daily
Crown of thorns (*Euphorbia splendens*)	Bright indirect	Water well when surface dries	Stem cuttings	Has pinkish-white, rose, red, or coral flowers
Diffenbachia nickname: dumb cane	Bright, indirect or filtered	Water well when surface dries	Air layering	Leaves contain acrid sap that causes loss of voice. Wash hands well after handling plant.
Dizygotheca (*Dizygotheca elegantissima*) nickname: false aralia	Bright indirect or filtered	Water well when surface dries	Division	Supply good drainage to avoid leaf drop
Dracaena Red-margined dracena Corn plant Warneckei dracena	Bright indirect or filtered	Evenly moist soil	Air layering or division	Many species available—most are variegated; colors include red, pink, yellow, and white
Fatsia (*Fatsia japonica*)	Bright indirect	Evenly moist soil	Stem cuttings	Pinch tops to induce dense growth
Ferns:				
Bird's-nest fern (*Asplenium* sp.)	Bright indirect	Evenly moist soil	Division	Water staghorn fern by placing it in the shower twice a week. Propagate by removing offset: back each with a ball of sphagnum and tie to a board
Boston fern (*Nephrolepis* sp.)	Bright indirect	Evenly moist soil	Division	
Brake fern (*Pteris* sp.)	Bright indirect	Evenly moist soil	Division	
Hare's-foot fern (*Polypodium* sp.)	Bright indirect	Evenly moist soil	Division	
Holly-fern (*Cyrtomium* sp.)	Bright indirect	Evenly moist soil	Division	
Lacy fern (*Asplenium* sp.)	Bright indirect	Evenly moist soil	Division	
Maidenhair fern (*Adiantum* sp.)	Filtered	Evenly moist soil	Division	
Rabbit's-foot fern (*Davallia* sp.)	Bright indirect	Evenly moist soil	Division	
Staghorn fern (*Platycerium* sp.)	Bright indirect	Evenly moist soil		
Ficus Fiddleleaf fig Weeping fig Rubber plant	Bright indirect	Evenly moist soil	Air layering	Many varieties available; some may grow to tree size in several years
Fittonia	Bright indirect or filtered	Evenly moist soil	Stem cuttings	Prefers porous soil, high in humus

FAVORITE INDOOR PLANTS

COMMON NAME	LIGHT	WATER	PROPAGATION	COMMENTS
Hoya (*Hoya carnosa*)	Bright indirect	Water well when surface dries	Stem cuttings	White blooms appear in one or two years
Ivy & ivy-like vines: English ivy (*Hedera* sp.) German ivy (*Senecio* sp.) Grape ivy (*Cissus* sp.) Swedish ivy (*Plectranthus* sp.)	Bright indirect Bright indirect Bright indirect Bright indirect	Evenly moist soil Evenly moist soil Evenly moist soil Evenly moist soil	Stem cuttings Stem cuttings Stem cuttings Stem cuttings	Mist foliage daily to discourage red spider mites, especially on English ivy
Jade plant (*Crassula argentea*)	Sunny or bright indirect	Keep on dry side	Air layering	Pink flowers may appear in fall
Maranta (*Maranta leuconeura*) nickname: prayer plant	Bright indirect or filtered	Evenly moist soil	Division	Keep soil on dry side in winter
Mimosa (*Mimosa pudica*) nickname: sensitive plant	Filtered	Evenly moist soil		Start plants from seed
Monstera (*Monstera deliciosa*)	Bright indirect or filtered	Evenly moist soil	Air layering or stem cuttings	To propagate, stick aerial roots in soil
Moses-in-a-boat (*Rhoeo spathacea*)	Bright indirect or filtered	Evenly moist soil		Remove suckers and pot up
Norfolk Island pine (*Araucaria heterophylla*)	Bright indirect	Water well when surface dries	Stem cuttings	Water less in winter
Orchids: Cattleya Cymbidium Lady-slipper Moth orchid	Sunny Sunny Bright indirect Bright indirect	Evenly moist soil Evenly moist soil Evenly moist soil Evenly moist soil	Division Division Division Division	Pot up orchids in fir bark or tree-fern chunks (osmunda). Mist foliage daily in the morning
Palms: Areca (*Chrysalidocarpus* sp.) Bamboo palm (*Chamaedorea or Rhapis*) Fishtail palm (*Caryota* sp.) Howea palm (*Howeia* sp.) Lady palm (*Rhapis* sp.) Parlor palm (*Chamaedorea* sp.) Sago palm (*Cycas* sp.)	Bright indirect Bright indirect Bright indirect Bright indirect Bright indirect Bright indirect Bright indirect	Water well when surface dries Water well when *surface dries* Water well when surface dries Water well when surface dries Water well when surface dries Water well when surface dries Water well when surface dries		Mist foliage daily and trim off brown leaf tips; palms are difficult to *propagate—buy young* plants to increase your collection
Pandanus nickname: screw pine	Bright indirect	Water well when surface dries		Remove and pot up offsets

✿ FAVORITE INDOOR PLANTS ✿

COMMON NAME	LIGHT	WATER	PROPAGATION	COMMENTS
Peperomia	Bright indirect	Evenly moist soil	Leaf cuttings or stem cuttings	Water less in winter
Philodendron	Bright indirect or filtered	Evenly moist soil	Stem cuttings	Both vining and self-heading kinds available
Pickaback plant (*Tolmiea menziesi*)	Bright indirect	Evenly moist soil	Runners or leaf cuttings	Plantlets appear atop mature leaves
Pilea	Bright indirect	Evenly moist soil	Stem cuttings or division	Good terrarium or tabletop plant
Pittosporum (*Pittosporum tobira*)	Bright indirect	Water well when surface dries	Air layering or stem cuttings	Prune back in spring before new growth appears
Pleomele	Bright indirect	Evenly moist soil	Stem cuttings	Will grow in water as well as in soil
Podocarpus	Sunny or bright indirect	Evenly moist soil	Stem cuttings	Prune in early spring for denser growth
Ponytail (*Beaucarnea recurvata*)	Sunny or bright indirect	Water well when surface dries		Start new plants from seeds
Pothos	Bright indirect	Water well when surface dries	Stem cuttings	Good office plant
Purple passion (*Gynura* sp.)	Sunny	Evenly moist soil	Stem cuttings	Prune stem ends for denser growth
Sansevieria nickname: snake plant	Bright indirect	Keep on dry side	Leaf cuttings or division	May bloom if pot-bound
Spathiphyllum (*Spathiphyllum patini*)	Bright indirect	Evenly moist soil	Division	Has a flower similar to calla lily
Strawberry saxifrage	Bright indirect	Water well when surface dries	Runners	Dainty white flowers in summer
Succulents (including cactus)	Sunny	Keep on dry side	Stem cuttings	Prefers porous soil and good drainage
Trileaf wonder (*Syngonium podophyllum*)	Bright indirect	Evenly moist soil	Stem cuttings	Pinch back to keep plant within bounds
Waffle plant (*Hemigraphis* sp.)	Bright indirect	Evenly moist soil	Stem cuttings	Spreading plant good for hanging baskets or as a ground cover in planters
Wandering Jew (*Tradescantia* sp. or *Zebrina* sp.)	Bright indirect	Evenly moist soil	Stem cuttings	East sun intensifies coloration of foliage
Zebra plant (*Aphelandra* sp.)	Bright indirect	Water well when surface dries	Stem cuttings	A bit touchy to grow, but worth the effort

Summer Vacations for Indoor Plants

Houseplants—like all other plants—are natives of the outdoors, and it's only proper they spend summers in their natural home. The sunshine and fresh air provide a more comfortable environment than a stuffy room indoors. Because your houseplants should already be properly potted in containers, the only problem with moving them outdoors will be finding the right spot.

Select a place that is shady and protected from strong wind. A porch, balcony, or a corner of your patio or deck are good possibilities. Some plants—such as cactus and succulents and indoor citrus trees—can tolerate bright sun, but most plants prefer dappled light or shade. Ferns and other delicate plants need fairly deep shade.

Move plants outdoors when temperatures are dependably warm and nights don't fall below 60 degrees.

To ease the stress of moving plants outdoors, make the transition gradually. If you have just a few containers, bring them outdoors each morning, then carry them back inside before the afternoon sun becomes strong. In several days, plants will be fully adjusted. If you have too many plants to bother moving them in and out, wait for a cloudy (but not a rainy) day. Then set them all outdoors in fairly strong shade. Several days later they can be moved to the permanent summer location you've picked.

Sunburn and wind damage are the first problems plants may encounter as they adjust to their new climate. To lessen these dangers, check the plants often and move them into deeper shade if they show signs of sunburn. Protect plants from wind by setting them behind shrubs or trees.

A lattice-protected sun porch is an excellent place for indoor plants to spend their summer.

This movable plant stand is easy to build from 2x4s; it has space for hanging plants and potted specimens.

Summer Vacations for Indoor Plants

Indoor plants will become an integral part of your outdoor living area with a special structure to house them for the summer. The structure can be as simple as a knock-down trellis or as elaborate as the lath house shown below. In climates where plants can be left outdoors most of the year, a lath house, gazebo, or similar structure is an especially good investment. It will provide protection from hot sun, strong winds, and driving rains yet will allow the benefits of filtered sunshine, good air circulation, and natural rainfall.

Plants are always happiest when they're grouped together (as shown in the photograph at right), so they can establish their own microclimate. They protect each other from harsh weather and share humidity and warmth when night temperatures become cool. Even if you don't have a special structure for your plants, keep them grouped in their own special area, such as a protected corner of your porch or patio.

The first two weeks your plants are outdoors, check them frequently to see if they need water—then, as you become accustomed to the amount each needs, you can establish a regular watering schedule. Plants in clay pots will dry out more quickly than those in plastic; when temperatures are extremely hot, they may need to be watered daily.

One of the best ways to water—and add humidity at the same time—is to use a gentle spray from a garden hose. The hose will duplicate a natural summer shower, and left-over water will simply drain away. The floor in this lath house is a bed of ½-inch gravel, three to four inches deep. Excess water can drain into the gravel and evaporate, raising the humidity around the plants.

This lovely lath house provides a perfect environment for summering plants outdoors.

Inside the lath structure, colorful flowering plants are grouped together in a rock garden.

Summer Vacations for Indoor Plants

You can build a simple structure to display, as well as protect, indoor plants that are outdoors for the summer by using a wall of your house or garage. In the photograph below, an extended lattice overhang along a garage wall provides space for a collection of gloxinias and other blooming plants. A summer respite outdoors can often prompt reluctant plants into flower. And because gloxinias and other blooming plants are easily damaged by wind and rain, the overhead lath is narrowly spaced to provide as much protection as possible.

When heavy rains, wind, or hail are predicted, plants should be brought indoors immediately. But you should leave them out during normal sum-mer rains—natural, untreated rain-water is very good for them. You may even want to set out a pail or bucket to catch rain to use for watering.

Bringing plants indoors during a storm would be no chore with the lattice addition to the home at right. The plants are just a few feet away from total protection. Because they're so close to the house, it's a simple matter to rotate plants to the indoors to make space for others. Plants will grow very quickly once they're outside; you may need to bring them in periodically to cut back.

Because plants will grow quickly over the summer, feed them fairly often to make sure new growth is vigorous. Use a standard houseplant fertilizer.

Gloxinias and other blooming plants take shelter outdoors under a lath roof and add interest to a neglected corner.

A lattice addition off the dining room of this house provides protection for bromeliads and other plants.

INDEX